Ecosystems as Natural Assets

Ecosystems as Natural Assets

Edward B. Barbier

Department of Economics & Finance
University of Wyoming
USA

ebarbier@uwyo.edu

the essence of knowledge

Boston – Delft

Foundations and Trends® in Microeconomics

Published, sold and distributed by:
now Publishers Inc.
PO Box 1024
Hanover, MA 02339
USA
Tel. +1-781-985-4510
www.nowpublishers.com
sales@nowpublishers.com

Outside North America:
now Publishers Inc.
PO Box 179
2600 AD Delft
The Netherlands
Tel. +31-6-51115274

The preferred citation for this publication is E. B. Barbier, Ecosystems as Natural Assets, Foundations and Trends® in Microeconomics, vol 4, no 8, pp 611–681, 2008

ISBN: 978-1-60198-286-5
© 2009 E. B. Barbier

Foundations and Trends® in Microeconomics

Volume 4 Issue 8, 2008

Editorial Board

Editorial Scope

Foundations and Trends® in Microeconomics will publish survey and tutorial articles in the following topics:

- Environmental Economics
- Contingent Valuation
- Environmental Health Risks
- Climate Change
- Endangered Species
- Market-based Policy Instruments
- Health Economics
- Moral Hazard
- Medical Care Markets
- Medical Malpractice
- Insurance economics
- Industrial Organization
- Theory of the Firm
- Regulatory Economics
- Market Structure
- Auctions
- Monopolies and Antitrust
- Transaction Cost Economics
- Labor Economics
- Labor Supply
- Labor Demand
- Labor Market Institutions
- Search Theory
- Wage Structure
- Income Distribution
- Race and Gender
- Law and Economics
- Models of Litigation
- Crime
- Torts, Contracts and Property
- Constitutional Law
- Public Economics
- Public Goods
- Environmental Taxation
- Social Insurance
- Public Finance
- International Taxation

Information for Librarians

Foundations and Trends® in Microeconomics, 2008, Volume 4, 8 issues. ISSN paper version 1547-9846. ISSN online version 1547-9854. Also available as a combined paper and online subscription.

Foundations and Trends® in
Microeconomics
Vol. 4, No. 8 (2008) 611–681
© 2009 E. B. Barbier
DOI: 10.1561/0700000031

Ecosystems as Natural Assets

Edward B. Barbier

Department of Economics & Finance, University of Wyoming, USA
ebarbier@uwyo.edu

Abstract

It is now standard in economics to model natural resources as a special
form of capital that can be depleted or accumulated. The following
review shows how such an approach can be extended to ecosystems,
implying that they are a form of natural asset that produces a flow of
beneficial goods and services over time. The review includes a discussion
of valuing ecosystem services, focusing on the problem of benefits
that vary spatially across landscapes and illustrated with the example
of coastal ecosystems. The starting point of the basic natural asset
model is the assumption that any ecological landscape that is conserved
must compete with other assets in the portfolio of wealth owners in the
economy. The model shows the importance of valuing ecosystem services
to the optimal allocation of landscape among competing uses.
It includes the possibility of an ecological transition, when it becomes
technologically feasible to restore developed land as ecological landscape.
The basic model is then extended to allow for the value of an
ecosystem service and the costs of maintaining this service to vary with
the spatial distance across the natural landscape; for the implications
when the economy is opened to trade; and finally, for examining the
effects of the risk of ecological collapse.

Contents

1

Introduction

An important contribution of natural resource economics has been to treat the natural environment as a form of capital asset (Clark and Munro, 1975; Dasgupta and Heal, 1974, 1979; Scott, 1955; Smith, 1968). The more recent literature on ecosystem services implies that these environmental systems can also be viewed as *natural assets* that produce a flow of beneficial goods and services over time (Barbier, 2007; Daily, 1997; Heal et al., 2005; Millennium Ecosystem Assessment, 2005; Pagiola et al., 2004; World Resources Institute, 2001). The purpose of the following review is to explore this literature and related modeling to show explicitly how the concept of ecosystems as natural assets translates into the traditional "natural capital" approach of resource economics.

An immediate barrier to such an approach is that, in ecology, the concept of an ecosystem has been difficult to define or to measure quantitatively (O'Neill, 2001; Pickett and Cadenasso, 2002). However, some ecologists suggest that most ecological processes are influenced by the spatial extent, or *landscape*, that defines the boundary of the system (Bockstael, 1996; O'Neill, 2001; Perry, 2002; Pickett and Cadenasso, 1995, 2002; Turner, 2005; Zonneveld, 1989). As shown in this review, by adopting ecological landscape, or land area, as the basic unit, modeling the ecosystem as a natural asset is relatively straightforward. Integrated economy-ecosystem models have started using a similar starting point, to examine human transformation of an ecological landscape through land use conversion, leaving the residual land for ecological processes and habitat for species (Brock and Xepapadeas, 2002; Eichner and Pethig, 2006; Finnoff et al., 2008; Tschirhart, 2000). But whereas these integrated models focus on modeling the complex ecological processes and feedback effects on multiple ecosystem services that arise through land conversion, the approach in the following review is to adopt a much simpler model of land use change. Such models of competing land use have been employed in many contexts to analyze the allocation of land between alternative uses (Amacher et al., 2009; Barbier and Burgess, 1997; Benhin and Barbier, 2001; Crocker, 2005; Hartwick et al., 2001; McConnell, 1989; Parks, 1995; Parks et al., 1998; Rowthorn and Brown, 1999; Stavins and Jaffe, 1990).

In applying competing land use models to ecosystems, the starting point is the assumption that the amount of an ecological landscape that is preserved must compete with other assets in the portfolio of wealth owners in the economy. The remaining landscape area yields a flow of ecosystem services, which have value but are non-marketed. The first version of the basic model considers a one-time irreversible development of the landscape. Land that is converted and developed has a market value, and the rate of appreciation of land awaiting development must equal the opportunity cost of the land investment, which includes an adjustment for the ratio of the value of ecosystem services to the capital value of the developed land. This basic model is extended to the case of continuous conversion of the ecological landscape over time, taking into account the costs of converting land and any capital gains from increases in the value of unconverted land. The model is solved to show the conditions under which a positive amount of ecosystem land is conserved rather than converted to commercial use. Finally, the basic model examines the case of a possible *ecological transition*, whereby it becomes technologically feasible to restore developed land as ecological landscape, leading to a new phase of land use in which ecological restoration occurs.

Three further extensions to the natural asset model are developed in this review.

The first extension examines the case in which both the value of an ecosystem service and the costs of maintaining this service vary with the spatial distance across the natural landscape of an ecosystem. This geographical variation may be due to the biophysical functioning of the ecosystem that generate different services at different locations across the landscape, and also due to the higher costs incurred of maintaining a larger landscape area. Allocating natural landscape now becomes a spatial problem. To avoid landscape conversion, at each location the marginal willingness to pay for the ecosystem services must be sufficiently large to offset the maintenance cost of those services at that location and the marginal opportunity cost of foregone rents from developing the entire landscape. This condition is less likely to hold if there is any "spatial" discounting effect due to the unidirectional decline of ecological functions across the landscape.

The second extension looks at the implications to the model when the economy is opened to trade. It is shown that rising terms of trade lead to two opposite effects. There will be increased land conversion as exports of the marketed production from converted land become more profitable. However, if imports are a substitute for domestic consumption of the marketed output, then there is less pressure to increase land conversion. Thus the impacts on the amount of ecosystem land conserved are ambiguous, as are the effects on overall welfare. In comparison, an international transfer, in the form of *payment for ecosystem services*, slows down the initial conversion of natural landscape, and encourages more landscape conversion in the long run.

The last extension examines the vulnerability of the ecosystem to collapse as land conversion proceeds. Following Reed and Heras (Reed and Heras, 1992) the risk of ecosystem collapse is modeled as a hazard rate function, where the hazard rate is defined as the probability at any time t that the ecosystem will collapse given that it has not collapsed up until that time period. The stochastic optimization problem is converted to a more tractable deterministic control problem and solved for the conditions determining the risk of collapse.

The outline of the review is as follows. Section 2 discusses ecosystem services and ecological landscapes as the basis of representing ecosystems as a natural asset. Simple two-period diagrammatic examples of the conversion of an area of coastal zone to commercial development are used to illustrate the basic concepts and issues. The section ends with the example of valuing ecosystem services of mangroves in Thailand to show how such valuation can influence both the decision to convert mangrove landscapes to shrimp aquaculture and whether or not to restore mangrove ecosystems after shrimp ponds are abandoned. Section 3 develops the basic natural asset model of an ecosystem by employing the competing land use model. The first version of the model considers a one-time irreversible development of an ecological landscape. The second version examines continuous conversion of the ecological landscape over time, and is extended to allow for an *ecological transition* where restoration is feasible. Section 4 begins by returning the example of coastal landscapes and discusses ecological evidence that the basic functions of these systems are spatially variable. Evidence of spatial heterogeneity of landscapes is explored further, with the example of non-linear wave attenuation across a mangrove landscape that affects the value of the coastal protection service and how it affects the mangrove-shrimp farm competing use problem in Thailand. The section ends by demonstrating how a spatial model of allocating natural landscape can be developed to incorporate some of these features of geographical variation of ecological functions. Section 5 revisits the basic natural asset model of competing uses of an ecological landscape and extends it to an open economy setting. The extension allows for consideration of trade interventions versus international payments for ecosystem services as incentives for greater ecosystem conservation. Section 6 extends the basic model to consider the problem of ecological collapse, and shows that more of the ecological landscape will be preserved compared to when the threat of collapse is absent. Section 7 concludes the review.

2

Ecosystem Services and Ecological Landscapes

2.1 What are Ecosystem Services?

Broadly defined, "ecosystem services are the benefits people obtain from ecosystems" (Millennium Ecosystem Assessment, 2005, p. 53). Such benefits are typically described by ecologists in the following manner: "Ecosystem services are the conditions and processes through which natural ecosystems, and the species that make them up, sustain and fulfill human life. ... In addition to the production of goods, ecosystem services are the actual life-support functions, such as cleansing, recycling, and renewal, and they confer many intangible aesthetic and cultural benefits as well." (Daily, 1997, p. 3). Thus in the current literature the term "ecosystem services" lumps together a variety of "benefits", which in economics would normally be classified under three different categories: (i) *goods* (e.g., products obtained from ecosystems, such as resource harvests, water and genetic material), (ii) *services* (e.g., recreational and tourism benefits or certain ecological regulatory functions, such as water purification, climate regulation, erosion control, etc.), and (iii) *cultural benefits* (e.g., spiritual and religious, heritage, etc.).

Regardless how one defines and classifies ecosystem services, as a report from The US National Academy of Science has emphasized, "the fundamental challenge of valuing ecosystem services lies in providing an explicit description and adequate assessment of the links between the structure and functions of natural systems, the benefits (i.e., goods and services) derived by humanity, and their subsequent values" (Heal et al., 2005, p. 2). Moreover, it has been increasingly recognized by economists and ecologists that the greatest "challenge" they face is in valuing the ecosystem services provided by key ecosystem *regulatory and habitat functions*. Table 2.1 provides some examples of the links

Table 2.1.   Some services provided by ecosystem regulatory and habitat functions.

Ecosystem functions	Ecosystem processes and components	Ecosystem services (benefits)
Regulatory Functions		
Gas regulation	Role of ecosystems in biogeochemical processes	Ultraviolet-B protection Maintenance of air quality Influence of climate
Climate regulation	Influence of land cover and biologically mediated processes	Maintenance of temperature, precipitation
Disturbance prevention	Influence of system structure on dampening environmental disturbance	Storm protection Flood mitigation
Water regulation	Role of land cover in regulating runoff, river discharge and infiltration	Drainage and natural irrigation Flood mitigation Groundwater recharge
Soil retention	Role of vegetation root matrix and soil biota in soil structure	Maintenance of arable land Prevention of damage from erosion and siltation
Soil formation	Weathering of rock and organic matter accumulation	Maintenance of productivity on arable land
Nutrient regulation	Role of biota in storage and recycling of nutrients	Maintenance of productive ecosystems
Waste treatment	Removal or breakdown of nutrients and compounds	Pollution control and detoxification
Habitat Functions		
Niche and refuge	Suitable living space for wild plants and animals	Maintenance of biodiversity Maintenance of beneficial species
Nursery and breeding	Suitable reproductive habitat and nursery grounds	Maintenance of biodiversity Maintenance of beneficial species

Source: Adapted from Heal et al. (2005, Table 3.3).

between regulatory and habitat functions and the ecosystem services that ultimately benefit humankind.

2.2 Ecosystems as Natural Assets

The literature on ecological services implies that ecosystems are assets that produce a flow of beneficial goods and services over time (Barbier, 2007; Daily, 1997; Heal et al., 2005; Millennium Ecosystem Assessment, 2005; Pagiola et al., 2004; World Resources Institute, 2001). In this regard, they are no different from any other asset in an economy, and in principle, ecosystem services should be valued in a similar manner. That is, regardless of whether or not there exists a market for the goods and services produced by ecosystems, their social value must equal the discounted net present value (NPV) of these flows.

But the concept of an ecosystem is highly multi-dimensional and difficult to define or measure quantitatively (O'Neill, 2001; Pickett and Cadenasso, 1995). Recent developments in landscape ecology, however, suggest that the basic unit of most ecological processes is spatial and is synonymous with the land or *natural landscape* that defines the boundary of the system (Bockstael, 1996; O'Neill, 2001; Perry, 2002; Pickett and Cadenasso, 1995, 2002; Tsur and Zemel, 1994; Zonneveld, 1989). As summarized by Bockstael (1996, p. 1169) the implications for economic modeling of ecosystem processes and services are clear: "because landscape pattern and ecological processes are closely linked...land use change at one scale or another is perhaps the single greatest factor affecting ecological resources." In other words, as there are "reciprocal interactions between spatial pattern and ecological processes" (Turner, 2005, p. 319), it is the spatially heterogeneous area of landscape that is fundamental to the flow of beneficial goods and services that we now recognize as ecosystem services. If for each ecosystem we can define its corresponding landscape in terms of a quantifiable "land unit", which is defined as "a tract of land that is ecologically homogeneous at the scale level concerned" (Zonneveld, 1989, p. 68), then we have a representation of an ecosystem as a *natural asset* in the form of this unit of land, or ecological landscape.

For example, let us suppose that the flow of ecosystem services in any time period t, can be quantified and that we can measure what each individual is willing to pay for having these services provided to him or her. If we sum up, or aggregate, the willingness to pay by all the individuals benefiting in each period from the ecosystem services, we will have a monetary amount — call it B_t — which indicates the social benefits in the given time period t of those services. Hopefully, there will be a stream of such benefits generated by ecosystem services, from the present time and into the future. Because society is making a decision today about whether or not to preserve ecosystems, we want to consider the flow of benefits of these services, net of the costs of maintaining the natural ecosystems, in terms of their present value. To do this, any future net benefit flows are discounted into present value equivalents. In essence, we are treating natural ecosystems as a special type of capital asset — a kind of "natural wealth" — which just like any other asset or investment in an economy is capable of generating a current and future flow of income or benefits.

Compared to conventional economic or financial assets, environmental assets are subject to special measurement problems.

For one, these assets and services are a special type of "natural" capital (Just et al., 2004, p. 603). Ecosystems comprise the abiotic (nonliving) environment and the biotic (living) groupings of plant and animal species called communities. As with all forms of capital, when these two components of ecosystems interact, they provide a flow of services. If the ecosystem is left relatively undisturbed, then the flow services from the ecosystem's regulatory and habitat functions are available in quantities that are not affected by the rate at which they are used. Although like other assets in the economy an ecosystem can be increased by investment, such as through restoration activities, ecosystems can also be depleted or degraded, e.g., through habitat destruction, land conversion, pollution impacts and so forth.

Whereas the services from most assets in an economy are marketed, the benefits arising from the regulatory and habitat functions of ecosystems generally are not. If the aggregate willingness to pay for these benefits, B_t, is not revealed through market outcomes, then efficient management of such ecosystem services requires explicit methods to measure this social value.[1] In fact, the failure to consider the values provided by key ecosystem services in current policy and management decisions is a major reason for the widespread disappearance of many ecosystems and habitats across the globe (Millennium Ecosystem Assessment, 2005). The global expansion of human populations and economic activity are an important cause of this disappearance, due to among other things, increased demand for land, pollution or over-exploitation of resources (Kareiva et al., 2007; Millennium Ecosystem Assessment, 2005; UNEP, 2006; Valiela et al., 2001; Worm et al., 2006). The failure to measure explicitly the aggregate willingness to pay for otherwise non-marketed ecological services exacerbates these problems, as the benefits of these services are underpriced and may lead to excessive land conversion, habitat fragmentation, harvesting and pollution caused by commercial economic activity undertaken by humans.

Figure 2.1 illustrates the difficulty that the above challenges pose for managing ecosystems and their natural landscape optimally. In this

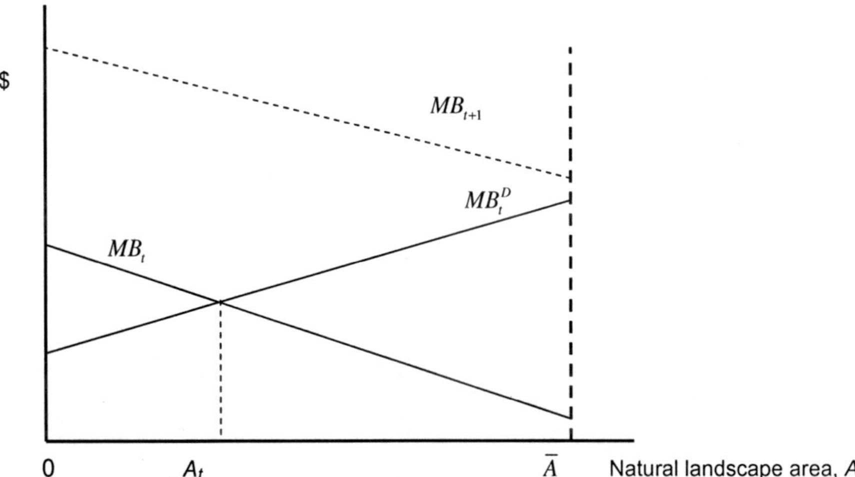

Fig. 2.1 Natural landscape conversion to development.

---

[1] However, standard economic valuation methods can be employed to measure the non-market value of many ecosystem services. For a review and further discussion, see (Barbier, 2007; Hanley and Barbier, 2009; Heal et al., 2005).

figure, the example of the conversion of an area of natural coastal landscape to commercial development is used.

In Figure 2.1, the marginal social benefits of ecological services at any time t are represented by the line MB_t for a coastal ecosystem of given area $\bar{A}$. For the purposes of illustration, this line is assumed to be downward-sloping, which implies that for every additional square kilometer of coastal landscape area, A, preserved in its original state, more ecosystem service benefits will be generated, but at a decreasing amount. A later section provides evidence supporting this assumption that marginal ecosystem benefits tend to decline in this way across a landscape, especially for some important services of coastal landscape (See Section 4). Note that it is straightforward to determine the aggregate willingness to pay for the benefits of these services, B_t, from this line; it is simply the area under the MB_t line. If there is no other use for the natural landscape, then the opportunity costs of maintaining it are zero, and B_t is at its maximum size when the entire coastal ecosystem is maintained at its original land area size $\bar{A}$. The ecosystem management decision is therefore simple; the coastal landscape should be completely preserved and allowed to provide its full flow of services in perpetuity.

However, population and economic development pressures in many areas of the world usually mean that the opportunity cost of maintaining coastal landscape is not zero. The ecosystem management decision needs to consider these alternative development uses of coastal landscape, which should be included in Figure 2.1. For example, suppose that the marginal social benefits of converting natural ecosystem land for these development options is now represented by a new line MB_t^D in the figure. Efficient land use now requires that $\bar{A} - A_t$ of coastal landscape should be converted for development leaving A_t of the original ecosystem undisturbed.

Both of the outcomes discussed so far assume that the willingness to pay for the marginal benefits arising from coastal ecosystem services, MB_t, is explicitly measured, or valued. But if this is not the case, then these non-marketed flows are likely to be ignored in the land use decision. Only the marginal benefits MB_t^D of the marketed outputs arising from coastal economic development activities will be taken into account, and as indicated in the figure, this implies that the entire ecosystem area $\bar{A}$ will be converted for development.

A further problem is the uncertainty over the future values of coastal landscape. It is possible, for example, that the benefits of ecosystem services are larger in the future as more scientific information becomes available over time. For example, suppose that in the subsequent period $t + 1$ it is discovered that the value of coastal ecosystem services is actually much larger, so that the marginal benefits of these services, MB_{t+1}, in present value terms is now represented by the dotted line in Figure 2.1. If the present value marginal benefits from coastal zone development in the future are largely unchanged, i.e., $\mathrm{MB}_t^D \approx M_{t+1}^D$, then as the figure indicates, the future benefits of ecosystem services exceed these costs, and the natural landscape should be restored to its original area $\bar{A}$, assuming of course that it is technically feasible and not excessively expensive to do so. Unfortunately, in making development decisions today we often do not know that, in the future, the value of ecosystem services will turn out to exceed development benefits. Our simple example shows that, if we have already made the decision today to convert $\bar{A} - A_t$ area of the natural landscape, then we will have to reverse this decision in the future period and restore the original coastal ecosystem.

Taking into account that future ecosystem service values are further complicated if development today leads to irreversible loss of natural landscape, or equivalently, ecological restoration of the landscape is prohibitively expensive. As pointed out by Krutilla and Fisher (1985), if environmental assets are irreversibly depleted, their value will rise relative to the value of other reproducible and accumulating economic assets. Such a scenario is likely for unique natural ecosystems and landscapes that are in fixed supply and are difficult to substitute for or restore, which implies that the beneficial services provided by their regulatory and habitat functions will decline over time as these assets are converted or degraded. Any decision today that leads to irreversible conversion therefore imposes a *user cost* on individuals who face a rising scarcity value of future ecosystem benefits as a consequence. This user cost should be part of a cost-benefit analysis of a

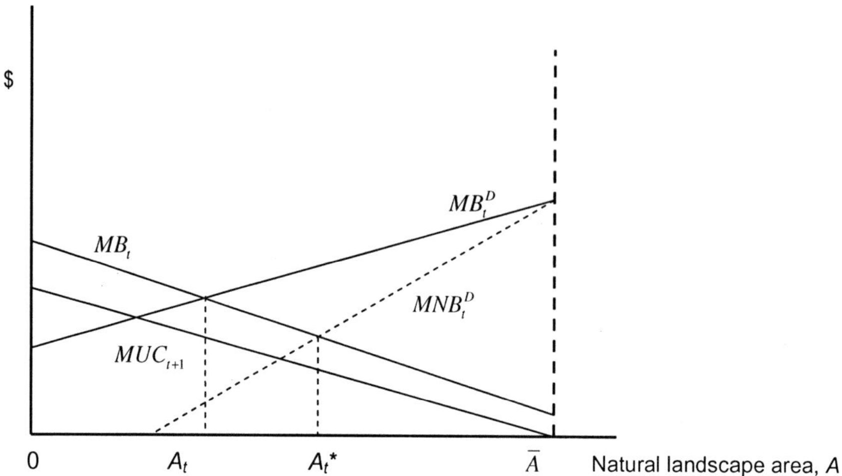

Fig. 2.2 Natural landscape conversion to development.

development proposal — but rarely is considered in actual natural landscape development decisions.

Figure 2.2 illustrates the additional measurement problem arising from irreversible conversion of fixed ecosystem assets.

As in the original example of Figure 2.1, if only the current benefits, MB_t, and opportunity costs, MB_t^D, of maintaining the original ecosystem are considered, then an amount $\bar{A} - A_t$ of natural landscape area would be converted today. But suppose that the loss of coastal ecosystem services arising from converting $\bar{A} - A_t$ causes the value of these services to rise. However, if ecosystem conversion is irreversible, then natural landscape area remains at A_t in time period $t + 1$. The resulting decline in welfare for individuals in the future is the user cost of irreversible loss of coastal and marine ecosystem services due to conversion today.[2] In Figure 2.2, the marginal user cost of development, measured

---

[2] Formally, let the change in natural landscape area over time be denoted as $A_{t+1} - A_t = f(d_t)$, where d_t represents the influence of development activities (e.g., conversion, degradation, etc.) in time t on the landscape area. If the "shadow value" that an increment of A_{t+1} would have over the remainder of the time horizon $(t + 1, \ldots, T)$ is defined as λ_{t+1}, then the expression $\lambda_{t+1} \partial f / \partial d_t$ explicitly reflects the influence of d_t on the value of the change in landscape area over time. If an increase in d_t reduces natural landscape area, then the latter expression indicates the user cost of landscape conversion.

in present value terms, is represented as the straight line MUC_{t+1}, which is zero when all the natural landscape is preserved but rises as more coastal land is converted. The correct land use decision should take into account this additional cost of irreversible ecosystem conversion due to expansion of coastal zone development today. Deducting the marginal user cost from MB_t^D yields the net marginal benefits of the development option, MNB_t^D. The latter is the appropriate measure of the opportunity costs of maintaining the ecological landscape, and equating it with the marginal social benefits of ecosystem services determines the intertemporally optimal landscape allocation. Only $\bar{A} - A_t^*$ of coastal ecosystem area should be converted for development leaving A_t^* of the original coastal ecosystem undisturbed.

Another problem of irreversible natural landscape conversion is that it can increase the risk of ecological collapse. Ecosystems tend to display non-convexities manifested through positive feedback interactions, which imply the presence of ecological thresholds (Batabyal et al., 2003; Dasgupta and Mäler, 2003; Elmqvist et al., 2003; Holling, 1973; Levin, 1999; May, 1975; Murray, 1993; Perrings, 1998; Pimm, 1984; Scheffer et al., 2001). That is, large shocks or sustained disturbances to ecosystems can set in motion a series of interactions that can breach ecological thresholds that cause the systems to "flip" from one functioning state to another. Although it is possible under certain conditions for the system to recover to its original state, under other conditions the change might be permanent. Thus, as (Dasgupta and Mäler, 2003, p. 501) remark, "if a large damage were to be inflicted on an ecosystem whose ability to function is conditional on it being above some threshold level (in size, composition, or whatever), the consequence would be irreversible." The inability of an ecosystem to recover, or return, its original state is essentially what is implied by an ecological collapse. Increasingly, ecologists have identified natural landscape conversion as one type of irreversible "large damage" that can increase the threat of ecosystem collapse (Busing and White, 1993; Dobson et al., 2006; Lotze et al., 2006; Peterson et al., 1998; Turner et al., 1993).

In Section 3, we incorporate many of the above characteristics of ecosystems as natural assets to develop a basic model of natural landscape allocation. Sections 4 and 5 extend the basic model to allow for spatial variation in the provision of an ecological function and open economy conditions, respectively. Section 6 addresses the issue of the risk of collapse from irreversible landscape conversion.

The remainder of this section illustrates the importance of valuing ecosystem services in landscape conversion and restoration decisions with the example of mangrove loss in Thailand.

2.3 Mangrove Land Use in Thailand

In Thailand, aquaculture expansion has been associated with mangrove ecosystem destruction. Since 1961 Thailand has lost from 1,500 to 2,000 km^2 of coastal mangroves, or about 50–60% of the original area (FAO, 2003). Over 1975–1996, 50–65% of Thailand's mangrove deforestation was due to shrimp farm conversion alone (Aksornkoae and Tokrisnam, 2004).

Mangrove deforestation in Thailand has focused attention on the two principle services provided by mangrove ecosystems, their role as nursery and breeding habitats for off-shore fisheries; and their role as natural storm barriers to periodic coastal storm events, such as wind storms, tsunamis, storm surges and typhoons. In addition, many coastal communities exploit mangroves directly for a variety of products, such as fuelwood, timber, raw materials, honey and resins, and crabs and shellfish. Various studies have suggested that these three benefits of mangroves are significant in Thailand (Barbier, 2003, 2007; Sathirathai and Barbier, 2001).

Valuation of the ecosystem services provided by mangroves is therefore important for two land use policy decisions in Thailand. First, although declining in recent years, conversion of remaining mangroves to shrimp farm ponds and other commercial coastal developments continues to be a major threat to Thailand's remaining mangrove areas. Second, since the December 2004 Indian Ocean tsunami, there is now considerable interest in rehabilitating and restoring mangrove ecosystems as natural barriers to future coastal storm events. Thus valuing the goods and services of mangrove ecosystems can help to address two important policy questions: do the net economic returns to shrimp farming justify further mangrove conversion to this economic activity,

Table 2.2. Comparison of land use values per ha, Thailand, 1996–2004 (US$).

Land use	Net present value per ha (10–15% discount rate)
Shrimp farming	
Net economic returns[a]	1,078–1,220
Mangrove ecosystem rehabilitation	
Total cost[b]	8,812–9,318
Ecosystem goods & services	
Net income from collected forest products[c]	484–584
Habitat-fishery linkage[d]	708–987
Storm protection service[e]	8,966–10,821
Total	10,158–12,392

Source: Barbier (2007).

[a]Based on annual net average economic returns US$322 per ha for five years from Sathirathai and Barbier (2001), updated to 1996$.

[b]Based on costs of rehabilitating abandoned shrimp farm site, replanting mangrove forests and maintaining and protecting mangrove seedlings. From Sathirathai and Barbier (2001), updated to 1996 US$.

[c]Based on annual average value of $101 per ha over 1996–2004 from Sathirathai and Barbier (2001), updated to 1996 US$.

[d]Based on a dynamic analysis of mangrove-fishery linkages over 1996–2004 and assuming the estimated Thailand deforestation rate of $3.44 \, \text{km}^2$ per year (see Barbier, 2007).

[e]Based on marginal value of expected damage avoided of $1,879 per ha from Barbier (2007).

and is it worth investing in mangrove replanting and ecosystem rehabilitation in abandoned shrimp farm areas?

To illustrate how improved and more accurate valuation of ecosystems can help inform these two policy decisions, Table 2.2 compares the per ha net returns to shrimp farming, the costs of mangrove rehabilitation and the value of mangrove services. All land uses are assumed to be instigated over 1996–2004 and are valued in 1996 US$ per hectare (ha).

Several analyses have demonstrated that the overall commercial profitability of shrimp aquaculture in Thailand provides a substantial incentive for private landowners to invest in such operations (Barbier, 2003; Sathirathai and Barbier, 2001; Tokrisna, 1998). However, many of the conventional inputs used in shrimp pond operations are subsidized, below border-equivalent prices, thus increasing artificially the private returns to shrimp farming. In Table 2.2 the net economic returns to shrimp farming, which are calculated once the estimated subsidies are removed, are based on non-declining yields over a five-year period of investment (Sathirathai and Barbier, 2001). After this period, there tends to be problems of drastic yield decline and disease; shrimp farmers then usually abandon their ponds and find a new location. In Table 2.2 the annual economic returns to shrimp aquaculture are estimated to be $322 per hectare (ha), and when discounted over the five-year period at a 10–15% rate yield a net present value of $1,078–$1,220 per ha.

There is also the problem of the highly degraded state of abandoned shrimp ponds after the five-year period of their productive life. Across Thailand those areas with abandoned shrimp ponds degenerate rapidly into wasteland, since the soil becomes very acidic, compacted and too poor in quality to be used for any other productive use, such as agriculture. To rehabilitate the abandoned shrimp farm site requires re-establishing tidal flows, treating and detoxifying the soil, replanting mangrove forests and maintaining and protecting mangrove seedlings for several years. As shown in Table 2.2, these restoration costs are considerable, $8,812–$9,318 per ha in net present value terms. This reflects the fact that converting mangroves to establish shrimp farms is almost an irreversible land use, and without considerable additional investment in restoration, these areas do not regenerate into mangrove forests. What should happen is that, before the decision to allow shrimp farming to take place, the restoration costs could be treated as one measure of the user cost of converting mangroves irreversibly, and this cost should be deducted from the estimation of the net returns to shrimp aquaculture. As the restoration costs exceed the net economic returns per ha, the decision should be to prevent the shrimp aquaculture operation from occurring.

Unfortunately, past land use policy in Thailand has ignored the user costs of shrimp farming, and as a result many coastal areas have been deforested of mangroves. Many short-lived shrimp farms in these areas have also long since fallen unproductive and are now abandoned. Thus, an important issue today is whether it is worth restoring mangroves in these abandoned areas. If the foregone benefits of the ecological services of mangroves are not large, then mangrove restoration may not be a reasonable option. Table 2.2 therefore indicates the value of three of these benefits: the net income from local mangrove forest products, habitat-fishery linkages and storm protection.

All three ecosystem services — coastal protection, wood product collection and habitat support for off-shore fisheries — have a combined value ranging from \$10,158–\$12,392 per hectare (ha) in net present value terms over the 1996–2004 period of analysis, and that the highest value of the mangrove by far is its storm protection service, which yields an annual benefit of \$1,879 per hectare (ha) annually, or a net present value of \$8,966–\$10,821. These ecosystem service values clearly exceed the net economic returns to shrimp farming. In fact, the net income to local coastal communities from collected forest products and the value of habitat-fishery linkages total to \$1,192–\$1,571 per ha, which are greater than the net economic returns to shrimp farming. However, the value of the storm protection is critical to the decision as to whether or not to replant and rehabilitate mangrove ecosystems in abandoned pond areas. As shown in Table 2.2, storm protection benefit makes mangrove rehabilitation an economically feasible land use option.

To summarize, this case study has shown the importance of valuing the ecological services in land use decisions, as outlined in Figures 2.1 and 2.2. The irreversible conversion of mangroves for aquaculture results in the loss of ecological services that generate significantly large economic benefits. This loss of benefits should be taken into account in land use decisions that lead to the widespread conversion of mangroves, but typically are ignored in private sector calculations. Finally, the largest economic benefits of mangroves appear to arise from regulatory and habitat functions, such as coastal storm protection and habitat-fishery linkages. This reinforces the importance of measuring the value of such ecological services.

3

The Basic Natural Asset Model

3.1 One-Time Development of a Natural Landscape

To illustrate further the natural asset properties of ecosystems, we consider the simplest problem of one-time development of an entire natural landscape to an alternative commercial use. Such a model turns out to have properties very similar to that of early economic models of land awaiting development that might have interim use or income (Arnott and Lewis, 1979; Shoup, 1970) or forest land that is clear cut once for timber but also yields non-timber benefits in the meantime (Hartman, 1976).

Let the initial landscape area of an ecosystem be denoted as A_0. If the landscape is completely converted and developed in its highest and best use at some future time t, then its value, expressed in terms of the optimal rent to developed land at that time, is $R(t)$. We assume that developed land is initially scarce in the economy, perhaps due to a large and growing population relative to the amount of available land, and thus the rental value of developed land increases over time, i.e., $R'(t) > 0$. But as more and more land conversion occurs throughout the economy, and because initially the best quality land for development is used first, $R''(t) < 0$. Also, until the natural landscape is converted at time t, it yields a flow of ecosystem services, or benefits. Denote the value of these benefits in each time period i as $B(i)$, which begin during the current period 0 and end at the time of development t. It follows that the present value of the landscape at time 0 is

$$V(t) = \max_t \left[R(t)e^{-rt} + \int_0^t B(i)e^{-ri}di \right] \tag{3.1}$$

The optimal date of development, t, is determined as

$$e^{-rt}\left[R'(t) - rR(t) + B(t)\right] = 0 \rightarrow R'(t) + B(t) = rR(t) \tag{3.2}$$

In Equation (3.2) $R'(t) + B(t)$ represents the gain from delaying development one period. It includes the increase in rental value of developed land plus the additional ecosystem benefits during that period of delay. The term $rR(t)$ represents the cost of delaying development. The value of the land, if sold in period t, could be invested to earn an interest income. The average interest rate on other assets in the economy is clearly key to the opportunity cost of delaying development another period. A higher interest rate means that it is costly to delay, whereas the lower interest rate has the opposite effect. Thus, although highly basic, condition (3.2) shows how the returns to holding on to ecosystems as a natural asset can be compared to the rate of return on other assets in the economy.

Condition (3.2) can also be written in the more familiar way

$$\frac{R'(t)}{R(t)} = r - \frac{B(t)}{R(t)} \tag{3.3}$$

Development should take place when the rate of change of development value of the land, $R'(t)/R(t)$, is equal to the interest rate, r, less the ratio of the ecosystem benefit flows per time period of the natural landscape to the development value of the land. As the rate of growth in the rental value of developed land is initially high but falls over time, condition (3.3) indicates that the net or effective interest rate is key to the decision as to whether or not to postpone development an additional period. With positive ecosystem benefits, $B(t)/R(t) > 0$, the effective interest rate is lower than the market rate, implying that the natural landscape should be developed when the rate of growth in its value is less than r, and thus development should be delayed.

Ecosystem benefits are therefore critically important to the optimal landscape development decision. When the benefits are large, development may not be optimal at all. First, as $B(t) \to \infty$, then the problem (3.1) is convex, and there is no feasible first-order condition for the optimal time for development. However, ecosystem benefits do not have to be that large for development to be delayed indefinitely. From Equation (3.2), if $R'(t) + B(t) > rR(t)$ for all t, then the gains from delaying development always exceed the costs, and the natural landscape should not be developed. Finally, if a solution for the optimal timing for development exists, it must also satisfy the second-order condition $R''(t) + B'(t) < rR'(t)$. If ecosystem benefits rise rapidly over time, perhaps because rapid development elsewhere in the economy has made such ecosystem services scare, then this condition might not be satisfied and there is no solution to Equation (3.1). Once again, development of the natural landscape should not occur.

Valuing ecosystem services as well as changes in this value over time is therefore important to determining the optimal time to develop natural landscape as well as whether or not development should take place at any time. As condition (3.3) indicates, the failure to value ecosystem benefits at all is tantamount to assuming that ecosystems are not natural assets. Their only value is as a potential source of developed land, and the development decision depends solely on comparing the growth in rental value to the market interest rate. Natural landscape development will take place too soon, if it should occur at all.

3.2 Continuous Conversion of a Natural Landscape

Although the natural landscape of an ecosystem might be completely converted through one-time development, a more likely scenario is that the landscape is subject to continuous but irreversible conversion to land used in economic development activities. Here, it is shown that this problem can be easily analyzed by employing a *competing land use model*, which has been used in many contexts to analyze the allocation of land between alternative uses (Amacher et al., 2009; Barbier and

Burgess, 1997; Benhin and Barbier, 2001; Crocker, 2005; Hartwick et al., 2001; McConnell, 1989; Parks, 1995; Parks et al., 1998; Rowthorn and Brown, 1999; Stavins and Jaffe, 1990).

In the following version of the problem, it is assumed that the land conversion decision is effectively irreversible because, once the ecological landscape is converted to another land use, the costs of restoring the landscape is either technically infeasible or prohibitively expensive relative to the ecosystem benefits obtained. Later in this section, this condition is modified to allow for the possibility of future restoration of the ecological landscape.

Let $A(t)$ be the area of natural ecosystem landscape at time t and $A(0) = A_0$ is the initial landscape area. If $c(t)$ is the area of natural landscape converted in each period to a development activity, then

$$A(t) = A_0 - \int_0^t c(s)ds \quad \text{and} \quad \dot{A} = -c(t) \tag{3.4}$$

It follows that, if $D(t)$ be the area of land use in the development activity and $D(0) = D_0$ is the initial developed land area, then

$$D(t) = D_0 + \int_0^t c(s)ds \quad \text{and} \quad \dot{D} = c(t) \tag{3.5}$$

Natural ecosystem landscape produces a flow of ecosystem services, or benefits, that vary across the landscape. Let $B(A(t))$ be the periodic ecosystem service flow from the remaining landscape area. These benefits vary non-linearly across the landscape such that $\partial B/\partial A(t) > 0$, $\partial^2 B/\partial A(t)^2 < 0$. Developed land is also heterogeneous in quality. Let R be the periodic rent associated with developed land. If the conversion decision is rational, then the highest quality land is allocated to development first, and differential rent will vary with land quality; i.e., there are decreasing marginal returns (rent) to the increase in the stock of developed land, $R(D(t))$, $\partial R/\partial D(t) > 0$, $\partial^2 R/\partial D(t)^2 < 0$. However, conditions (3.4) and (3.5) indicate that $D(t) = D_0 + A_0 - A(t)$. The latter expression implies in turn that the rents from developed land can be rewritten as $R(A(t))$, $\partial R/\partial A(t) < 0$.

If C are the costs of conversion, then more landscape conversion increases these costs, i.e., $C(c(t))$, $\partial C/\partial c(t) > 0$, $\partial^2 C/\partial c(t)^2 > 0$. It is also assumed that $C(0) = C'(0) = 0$.

The decision maker determining landscape use can maximize the present value of net returns from the land, V, by choosing optimal levels of land to convert, $c(t)$

$$\max_{c(t)} V = \int_0^\infty [R(D) - C(c) + B(A)]e^{-rt}dt \qquad (3.6)$$

subject to (3.4) and (3.5). However, if we use the above suggested substitutions in the expression for rent from developed land, then the current value Hamiltonian of the problem is

$$H = R(A) - C(c) + B(A) - \mu c,$$

where μ is the shadow value of natural landscape. Two of the first-order conditions of the problem are

$$\frac{\partial H}{\partial c} = 0 \rightarrow \mu = -C'(c) \qquad (3.7)$$

$$-\frac{\partial H}{\partial A} = \dot{\mu} - r\mu \rightarrow \dot{\mu} = r\mu - B'(A) - R'(A) \qquad (3.8)$$

Combining (3.7) and (3.8) yields

$$\begin{aligned}
-B'(A) - R'(A) &= \dot{\mu} + rC_c \rightarrow -R'(A) - rC'(c) \\
&= R'(D) - rC'(c) \\
&= B'(A) + \dot{\mu},
\end{aligned} \qquad (3.9)$$

where $-R_A = R_D$ is annual periodic rent from developed land use.

Condition (3.9) indicates that, along the optimal path of landscape conversion, the returns from the two competing land uses must be equal. The marginal profits from development less conversion costs $R'(D) - rC'(c)$ must equal the marginal benefit of holding on to the ecological landscape $B'(A) + \dot{\mu}$. Note that (3.9) can also be rewritten as

$$-\mu(t) = \frac{R'(D)}{r} - \frac{B'(A) + \dot{\mu}}{r} = C'(c).$$

The difference between the capitalized marginal value of developed land and land retained as ecological landscape is the marginal cost of converting landscape. Denote P as the "price", or capital value, of land that is associated with each of these respective capitalized land use values, then

$$\frac{R'(D)}{r} - \frac{B'(A) + \dot{\mu}}{r} = P(D(t)) - P(A(t)) = C'(c) \qquad (3.10)$$

The difference in land prices between developed and ecological land is the marginal cost of converting a unit of the ecological landscape into developed land.

In the long run steady state, $\dot{A} = \dot{\mu} = 0$. It follows from (3.4) and (3.7) that both landscape conversion and the marginal value of an additional unit of ecosystem landscape approach zero asymptotically, i.e., $c = 0$ and $\lim_{t \to \infty} \mu(t) = C_c(0) = 0$. The wedge between land prices will disappear, $P(D(t)) = P(A(t))$, and ecosystem landscape area will converge to a steady state level A^*.

Assume that the initial ecological landscape area is large $A(0) > A^*$. From (3.7), along the transition path to the long run steady state, the marginal value of an additional unit of ecosystem landscape is negative $\mu < 0$. Initially, optimal landscape conversion c is very large, which reflects the fact that developed land is relatively scarce compared to ecological landscape and essentially valued as a "reserve" to be converted for developed land. But because initial landscape area is large, the marginal value of ecosystem services from that landscape $B'(A)$ is very low whereas the marginal rent earned from developed land use $R'(D)$ is extremely high. The result is that the shadow value of ecological landscape $\mu(t)$ is rising over time. In fact, given that $A(0) > A^*$, along the optimal path until the steady state is reached, $\mu(t)$ continues rising and c falling.

Formally, from the necessary condition (3.7)

$$\partial\mu = -C''(c)\partial c \to \frac{\partial c}{\partial \mu} = -\frac{1}{C''(c)} < 0, \qquad (3.11)$$

which implies that Equation (3.4) can be written as $\dot{A} = -c(\mu)$ and confirms that, as the shadow value of natural landscape becomes less negative over time, optimal land conversion falls. The slope of the optimal path is

$$\frac{\partial\mu}{\partial A} = \frac{\dot{\mu}}{\dot{A}} = \frac{r\mu - B'(A) - R'(A)}{-c(\mu)} < 0, \qquad (3.12)$$

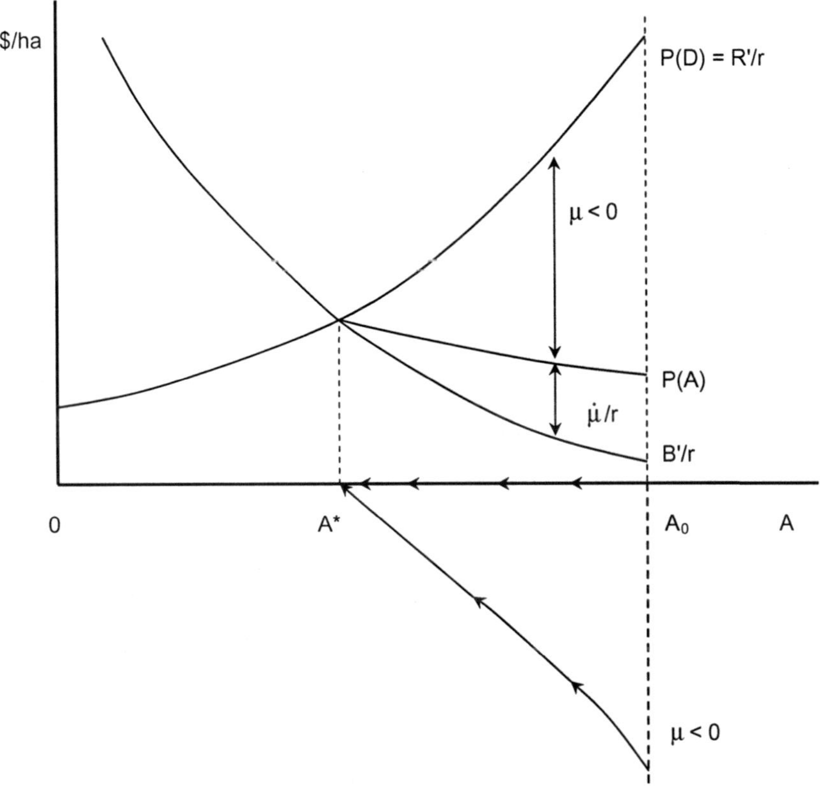

Fig. 3.1 Optimal landscape conversion in the basic model.

which verifies that, although initially natural landscape is very large, as land conversion proceeds and *A* falls, the shadow value of natural landscape becomes less negative. The optimal path for ecological landscape conversion is depicted in Figure 3.1.

However, as we have discussed previously, the problem for the decision maker determining landscape use is that markets do not take into account the value of nonmarket ecosystem services, so that typically $B'(A) = 0$ in most land use decisions. If that is the case, the only value of ecological landscape is as a "reserve" of developed land. Land will be developed until in the long run the entire landscape is converted $A^* = 0$ and $D^* = A_0$, and the capitalized value of land is zero, $R'(D^*)/r = \dot{\mu}/r = P(D^*) = 0$. This outcome is depicted in Figure 3.2.

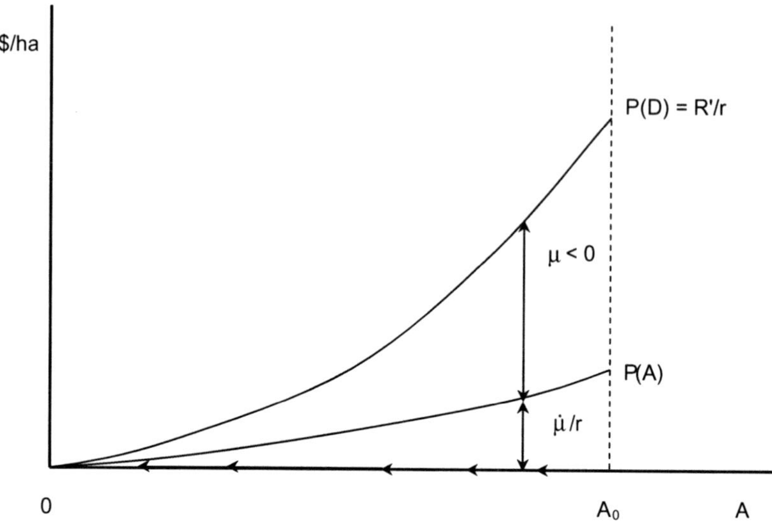

Fig. 3.2 Landscape conversion when ecosystem services are ignored.

3.3   An Ecological Transition

Although it might not be feasible initially to restore the natural land-scape, at some future time t_1, where $0 < t_1 < \infty$, it becomes technologically possible to restore developed land as ecological landscape. The value of restoring all developed land at time $t_1 \leq t \leq \infty$ can be denoted by the function $G(D(t)), G'(D(t)) > 0$.

At some finite time T, which occurs at the time or shortly after ecological restoration becomes feasible, i.e., $t_1 \leq T < \infty$, the future land rents earned from developed land are equal to the value of restoring all developed land at T

$$V(D(T)) = \int_T^\infty R(D(t))e^{-rt}dt = G(D(T)),$$

$$G'(D(T)) \geq V'(D(T)) > 0. \qquad (3.13)$$

Given that $D(t) = D_0 + A_0 - A(t)$ it follows that $V(D(T))$, which is the value of developed land from T onwards, can also be expressed as $V(A(T)), V'(A(T)) < 0$.

The competing land use model is now a finite time optimization problem with a designated terminal value associated with the stock of remaining ecological land at time T. The first order conditions of the model over the interval $[0, T]$ are the same as before, but the new transversality condition is

$$\mu(T) = -C'(c) = V'(A(T)) < 0. \tag{3.14}$$

At time T the marginal (negative) value of an additional stock of ecological landscape must equal the additional cost of converting it to developed land and also equal the marginal increase in future rents from developing another unit of the landscape.

From Equation (3.13) and using $-V'(A(T)) = V'(D(T))$ in (3.14), the transversality condition can also be written as

$$-\mu(T) = -V'(D(t)) \leq G'(D(T)) \tag{3.15}$$

where $-\mu(T)$ can be interpreted as the marginal value of an additional stock of developed land at T, which is equal to the marginal increase in the future rents from an additional unit of developed land. But this increase in the future stream of rents is equal to or less than the marginal value of restoring one unit of developed land at time T.

Two implications emerge from this transversality condition. First, conversion of ecological landscape to developed land will terminate at time T. Second, over the remaining time period $T \leq t \leq \infty$, a new phase of land use will occur involving the restoration of the stock of developed land to ecological landscape. Thus, the time period T denotes the *ecological transition* from development of ecological landscape to a period of ecological restoration.

Let $g(t)$ be the area of developed land restored in each period over $T \leq t \leq \infty$ to natural landscape. It follows that $A(t) = A_T + \int_T^t g(s)ds, A(T) = A_T$ and $\dot{A} = g(t)$. If $C(g)$ is the cost of restoration, which increases with the amount of land restored, i.e., $C'(g) > 0, C''(g) > 0, C(0) = C'(0) = 0$, then the maximization problem, from the standpoint of the beginning of the ecological transition, is now

$$\max_{g(t)} V = \int_T^\infty [R(A) + B(A) - C(g)]e^{-r(t-T)}dt, \text{ s.t. } \dot{A} = g, A(T) = A_T.$$

The current value Hamiltonian of the problem is $H = R(A) + B(A) - C(g) + \mu g$, which yields the following two necessary conditions

$$\frac{\partial H}{\partial c} = 0 \rightarrow \mu = C'(g) \tag{3.16}$$

$$-\frac{\partial H}{\partial A} = \dot{\mu} - r\mu \rightarrow \dot{\mu} = r\mu - B' - R_A \tag{3.17}$$

Combining Equations (3.16) and (3.17)

$$-R'(A) = R'(D) = B'(A) - rC'(g) + \dot{\mu} \tag{3.18}$$

$$\mu = \frac{B'(A) + \dot{\mu}}{r} - \frac{R'(D)}{r} = P(A) - P(D) = C'(g) \tag{3.19}$$

After the ecological transition, the difference between the capitalized marginal value of ecological landscape can also be designated as the difference in the "price" of ecological as opposed to developed land, but now this difference must be equivalent to the marginal cost of restoring a unit of developed land as ecological landscape.

In the long run steady state, $\dot{A} = \dot{\mu} = 0$ and $C'(0) = 0$. It follows that both landscape restoration and the marginal value of an additional unit of ecosystem landscape approach zero asymptotically, i.e., $g = 0$ and $\lim_{t \to \infty} \mu(t) = C'(0) = 0$. The wedge between land prices will disappear, $P(D(t)) = P(A(t))$, and ecosystem landscape area will converge to a steady state level A^{**}. If the initial landscape level is small, i.e., $D(T) > A(T) > A^{**}$ then from Equation (3.16), along the ecological restoration path to the long run steady state, the marginal value of an additional unit of ecosystem landscape is positive $\mu > 0$, and optimal landscape restoration g is very large, reflecting the fact that developed land is initially relatively abundant compared to ecological landscape. But because initial landscape area is small, the marginal value of ecosystem services from that landscape $B'(A)$ is very high whereas the marginal rent earned from developed land use $R'(D)$ is extremely low. The result is that the shadow value of ecological landscape $\mu(t)$ is falling over time. In fact, given that $A(T) < A^{**}$, along the optimal path until the steady state is reached, both $\mu(t)$ and g continue falling. The outcome is depicted in Figure 3.3.

Although the model of ecological transition developed here is relatively simple, it nonetheless captures two important aspects identified

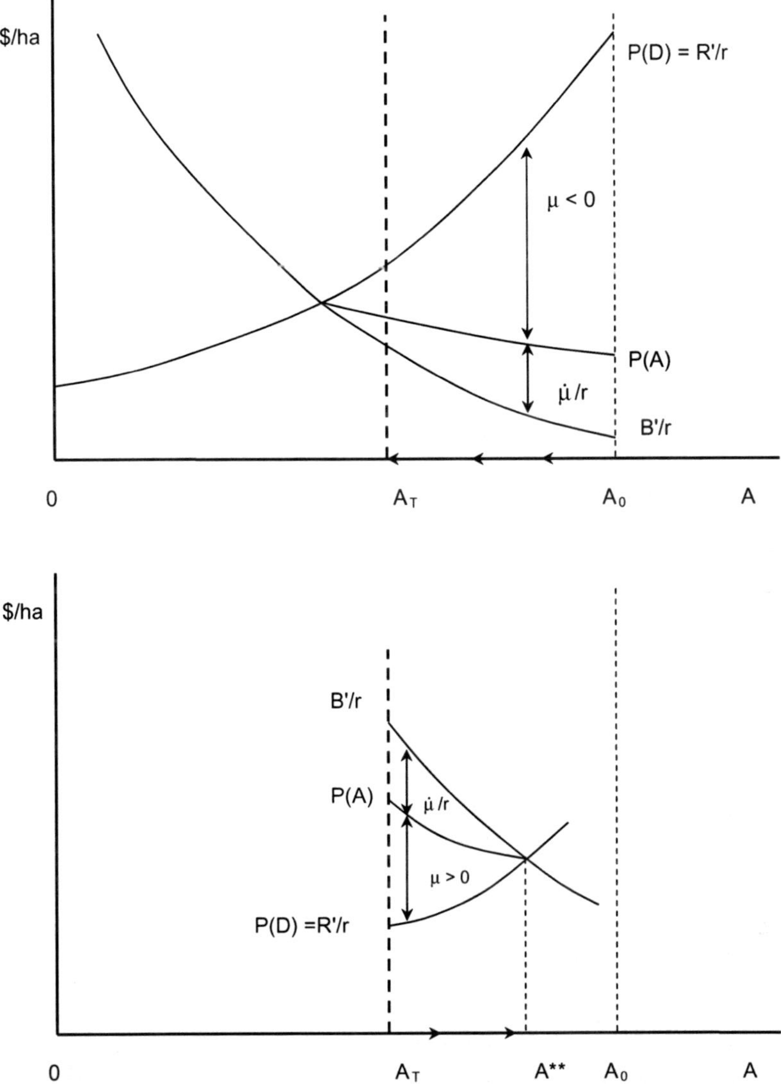

Fig. 3.3 The ecological transition and optimal landscape restoration.

in the literature: restoration must be technological feasible and the value of a restored ecological landscape must be sufficient to justify the costs of restoration. The notion that there may be distinct phases of ecological land use, where there is an initial phase irreversible landscape conversion takes place followed by a new phase where restoration is technically and economically feasible, is supported by the empirical literature on some key ecosystems.

For example, there is a longstanding *forest transition* literature, which emphasizes that a country's forest cover generally declines as it develops socially and economically, but eventually as an economy develops further, the increased demand for wood products and non-market ecosystem services from forested land may lead to forest replenishment, and perhaps eventually a recovery in the total forest area (Grainger, 1995, 2008; Kauppi et al., 2006; Mather, 1992, 2000, 2007; Palo and Vanhanen, 2000; Rudel et al., 2005; Walker, 1993).[3] Historical evidence of forest cover trends suggest that most of Western Europe, North America and the Pacific developed countries (e.g., Australia, Japan and New Zealand) underwent some from of transition in forest land use from decline to recovery in the nineteenth or early twentieth century. In recent years, there have also been some signs of similar forest recovery in some developing economies, notably Bangladesh, China, Costa Rica, Cuba, Dominican Republic, India, Morocco, Peninsular Malaysia, Puerto Rico, Rwanda, South Korea and Vietnam.

In comparison, ecological restoration of coastal, estuarine and marine systems has only received attention very recently [for reviews, see (Bosire et al., 2008; Elliott et al., 2007; Simenstad et al., 2006)]. As discussed in Section 2.3, for example, restoring mangroves on abandoned shrimp farm site is very costly, as it requires re-establishing tidal flows, treating and detoxifying the soil, replanting vegetation and maintaining and protecting mangrove seedlings for several years. Nevertheless, improvements in the technical feasibility of restoring estuarine hydrology and vegetation replanting methods have led to noticeable transitions to restoration of degraded and converted landscapes in locations where the services of these coastal ecosystems are especially valuable (Bosire et al., 2008; Dahdouh-Guebas et al., 2005; Elliott et al., 2007; Lewis III, 2000, 2005; Lewis III and Gilmore Jr, 2007; Reed and Wilson, 2004; Simenstad et al., 2006).

---

[3] For an economic explanation of why such transitions in long-run forest land use patterns may occur, see (Barbier et al., 2009).

4

Spatial Variation in Ecosystems

Since the seminal contribution by (Clark, 1976), economists have sought to develop spatial models of resource management in a variety of contexts, including renewable resource harvesting, deforestation, mining, biological invasion and marine reserve establishment (Albers, 1996; Alix-Garcia, 2007; Barbier, 2001; Brown and Roughgarden, 1997; Costello and Polasky, 2008; Gaudet et al., 2001; Kolstad, 1994; Robinson et al., 2008; Sanchirico and Wilen, 1999, 2005; Smith et al., 2009). The aim of the following section is also to show how spatial considerations matter in the treatment of ecosystems as natural assets. First, we return to the example of coastal landscapes and discuss ecological evidence that the basic functions of these systems are spatially variable. Evidence of spatial heterogeneity of landscapes is explored further, with the example of non-linear wave attenuation across a mangrove landscape that affects the value of the coastal protection service and how it affects the mangrove-shrimp farm competing use problem in Thailand. The section ends by demonstrating how a simple spatial model of allocating natural landscape can be developed to incorporate some of these features of geographical variation of ecological functions, thus affecting the location and extent of natural landscape conversion in an ecosystem.

4.1 Coastal Landscapes

Although most ecologists have concluded that ecosystem size and functional relationships are non-linear, the lack of data or mapping of these relationships has often precluded estimating how the value of an ecosystem service varies across an ecological landscape. However, studies of coastal systems suggest that, for a handful of key ecosystem services, it is possible to track how the ecological functions vary spatially and thus influence the economic benefits that they provide (Aburto-Oropeza et al., 2008; Aguilar-Perera and Appeldoorn, 2008; Barbier et al., 2008; Meynecke et al., 2008; Petersen et al., 2003; Peterson and Turner, 1994; Rountree and Able, 2007). What is more, much of the evidence suggests that benefits tend to decline with the distance inshore from the seaward edge of most coastal wetland habitats, such as mangroves and salt marshes.

For example, coastal interface systems, including mangroves, salt marshes, seagrass beds, nearshore coral reefs and sand dunes, can provide protection against wave damage caused by storms, hurricanes, tidal waves and other storm events, provided that such storm events are not too extreme in their magnitude (Barbier et al., 2008). However, for all these coastal habitats, non-linear landscape relationships exist between habitat area and measurements of the ecosystem function of wave attenuation. For mangroves and salt marshes, wave attenuation diminishes with increasing habitat distance inland from the shoreline. In the case of seagrasses and near-shore coral reefs, wave attenuation is a function of the water depth above the grass bed or reef, and these relationships are also nonlinear. There is also a spatial variable relationship between the percent cover of dune grasses and the size of oceanic waves blocked by the sand dunes produced by the grasses.

Coastal systems also strongly influence the abundance, growth and structure of neighboring marine fisheries by providing nursery, breeding and other habitat functions for commercially important fish and invertebrate species that spend at least part of their life cycles in coastal and estuarine environments. Evidence of this coastal habitat-fishery linkage is increasingly indicating that the value of this service is higher at the seaward edge or "fringe" of the coastal habitat than further inland (Aburto-Oropeza et al., 2008; Aguilar-Perera and Appeldoorn, 2008; Manson et al., 2005; Peterson and Turner, 1994). For example, Peterson and Turner (1994) find that densities of most fish and crustaceans were highest in salt marshes in Louisiana within 3 m of the water's edge compared to the interior marshes. In the Gulf of California, Mexico the mangrove fringe with a width of 5–10 m has the most influence on the productivity of near-shore fisheries, with a median value of \$37,500 per ha. Fishery landings also increased positively with the length of the mangrove fringe in a given location (Aburto-Oropeza et al., 2008).

To illustrate the influence of spatial variability on an ecosystem service and thus on the conversion of a coastal landscape for development, we return to the Thailand mangrove case study of Section 2.3. Recall that this study compared per hectare land use values between various mangrove ecosystem benefits and conversion of the mangrove to shrimp ponds in Thailand (see Table 2.2). But what if these per hectare values for mangroves were used to inform a land use decision weighing conversion of an entire mangrove ecosystem to shrimp aquaculture? For example, deciding how much of a mangrove forest extending 1000 m seaward along a 10 km coastline to convert to shrimp aquaculture may depend critically on whether or not all the mangroves in the $10 \, \text{km}^2$ ecosystem are equally beneficial in terms of coastal storm protection (Barbier et al., 2008).

Suppose that it is assumed initially that the annual per ha values for the various ecosystem benefits are spatially uniform, and thus vary linearly, across the entire $10 \, \text{km}^2$ mangrove landscape. Following this assumption, a mangrove area of $10 \, \text{km}^2$ would have an annual storm protection value of 1,000 times the \$1,879 per ha "point estimate", which yields an annual total benefit estimate of nearly \$1.9 million. Barbier et al. (2008) indicate how this assumption translates into a comparison of the net present value (10% discount rate and 20-year horizon) of shrimp farming to the three mangrove services — coastal protection, wood product collection and habitat support for off-shore fisheries — as a function of mangrove area (km^2) for the example of a $10 \, \text{km}^2$ coastal landscape. Figure 4.1 shows a comparison of these benefits.

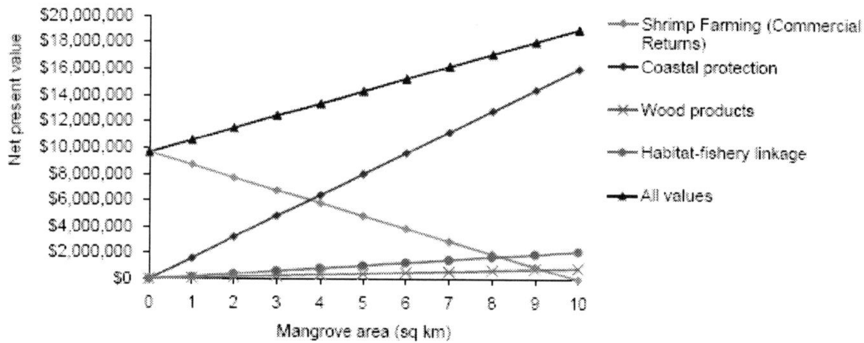

Fig. 4.1 Mangrove land use with spatially uniform ecosystem values.
Source: Barbier et al. (2008).

Figure 4.1 aggregates all four values to test whether an integrated land use option involving some conversion and some preservation yields the highest total value. When all values are linear, as shown in the figure, the outcome is a typical "all or none" scenario; either the aggregate values will favor complete conversion or they will favor preserving the entire habitat. Because the ecosystem service values are large and increase linearly with mangrove area the preservation option is preferred. The aggregate value of the mangrove system is at its highest ($18.98 million) when it is completely preserved, and any conversion to shrimp farming would lead to less aggregate value compared to full preservation, thus any land use strategy that considers all the values of the ecosystem would favor mangrove preservation and no shrimp farm conversion.

However, as discussed above, not all mangroves along a coastline are equally effective in storm protection. It follows that the storm protection value is unlikely to be uniform across all mangroves. The reason is that the storm protection "service" provided by mangroves depends on their critical ecological function in terms of "attenuation" of storm waves. That is, the ecological damages arising from tropical storms come mostly from the large wave surges associated with these storms. Ecological and hydrological field studies suggest that mangroves are unlikely to stop storm waves that are greater than 6 m (Alongi, 2008; Cochard et al., 2008; Forbes and Broadhead, 2007; Wolanski, 2007). On the other hand, where mangroves are effective as "natural barriers",

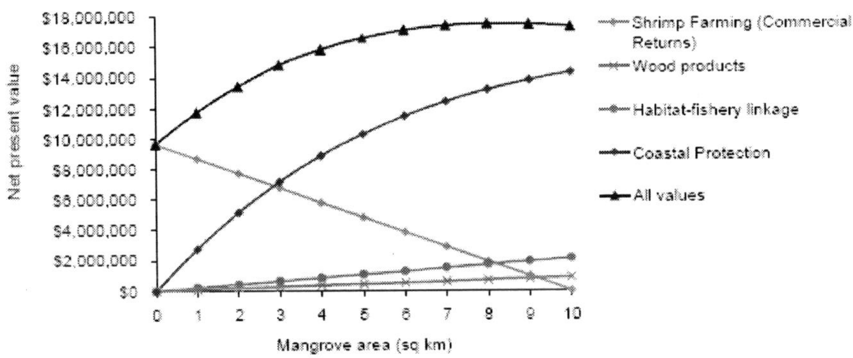

Fig. 4.2 Mangrove land use with spatially variable storm protection values.
Source: Barbier et al. (2008).

against storms that generate waves less than 6 m in height, the wave height of a storm decreases quadratically for each 100 m that a mangrove forest extends out to sea (Barbier et al., 2008; Mazda et al., 1997). In other words, wave attenuation is greatest for the first 100 m of mangroves but declines as more mangroves are added to the seaward edge.

Barbier et al. (2008) employ the non-linear wave attenuation function for mangroves based on the field study by Mazda et al. (1997) to revise the estimate of storm protection service value for the Thailand case study. The result is depicted in Figure 4.2.

The storm protection service of mangroves still dominates all values, but small losses in mangroves will not cause the economic benefits of storm buffering by mangroves to fall precipitously. The consequence is that the aggregate value across all uses of the mangroves, shrimp farming and ecosystem values, is at its highest ($17.5 million) when up to $2\,\mathrm{km}^2$ of mangroves are allowed to be converted to shrimp aquaculture and the remainder of the ecosystem is preserved.

Thus, taking into account how an ecological function varies spatially and influences the value of the ecosystem service it provides can have a significant impact on a land use decision at the landscape scale.

4.2 A Natural Landscape with Spatially Variable Benefits

As noted above, an interesting feature of some coastal ecosystems is that some of their key ecosystem services tend to vary unidirectionally across the system's natural landscape. For example, in the case of mangroves and salt marshes, both storm protection and habitat-fish linkage benefits tend to decline with the distance inshore from the seaward edge of most coastal wetland habitats, such as mangroves and salt marshes. The economic implications of such spatial variation in ecosystem functioning can be captured in a simple model that treats management of the natural landscape among competing uses as a spatial problem, following an approach similar to the spatial pricing problem developed by Takayama (1994).

For instance, assume that both the value of an ecosystem service and the costs of maintaining this service vary with the spatial distance across the natural landscape of an ecosystem. This geographical variation may be due to the biophysical functioning of the ecosystem that generate a different service at different locations across the landscape, and also due to the higher costs incurred of maintaining a larger landscape area. The distance across the landscape, and thus the service, can defined from one "edge" to a maximum boundary, i.e., $[0, A]$.

Let $S(A)$ be the total flow of ecosystem services over the entire spatial distance across the natural landscape of area, A. Thus $S(A)$ is defined as

$$S(A) = \int_0^A s(a)da, \tag{4.1}$$

where 0 denotes one ecologically defined boundary (e.g., the seaward edge of a coastal ecosystem) and A denotes the distance across to the furthest ecological boundary of the natural ecosystem landscape (e.g., the furthest landward edge of the coastal ecosystem. It is assumed that A is predetermined by the biophysical characteristics of the landscape. It follows from Equation (4.1) that $s(a)$ is the ecosystem service flow at any specific location, a, in the landscape.

We again want to consider the possibility that the natural landscape could have an alternative land use in some development activity. Denote the opportunity costs of maintaining the entire ecosystem landscape for service flow S as $C[S(A)]$. Since this opportunity cost is represented by the foregone rents that could be earned from developing the entire landscape, $R(A)$, then it follows that

$$C[S(A)] = R(A), \tag{4.2}$$

Now let $v(s(a))$ denote the marginal willingness to pay (WTP) for the benefits associated with the ecosystem service flow at each location, a. Associated with the marginal WTP is an implicit price

$$p(a) = v(s(a)). \tag{4.3}$$

The total WTP for the ecosystem service flow at location a is

$$V(s) = \int_0^s v(i)di. \tag{4.4}$$

To ensure a flow of ecosystem services requires some maintenance costs, e.g., to prevent encroachment, illegal conversion, overuse, etc. We assume that these costs, M, vary at each location a across the landscape, but if there is no longer any ecosystem, $M(0) = 0$. In addition, we represent maintenance costs as proportionate to the ecosystem service flow at each location; i.e., the higher the service flow, the more costs have to be expended to maintain it.

$$M(a) = m(a)s(a), M(0) = m(0) = 0. \tag{4.5}$$

It follows from Equation (4.1) that the change in total ecosystem services due to a marginal change in the landscape is related to the service flow at each location a. That is, differentiating Equation (4.1) with respect to A yields

$$\frac{\partial S}{\partial A} = s(A) \quad \text{and} \quad \dot{S}(a) = s(a) \quad \text{where} \quad \dot{S}(a) = \frac{\partial S}{\partial a}. \tag{4.6}$$

Note that integrating Equation (4.6) over the entire landscape distance $[0, A]$ yields Equation (4.1).

If a social planner could choose optimally the flow of ecosystem services at each location, $s(a)$, then the planner would choose it to maximize total net benefits over the entire ecosystem landscape

$$\max_{s(a)} W = \int_0^A [V(s(a)) - m(a)s(a)]da - R(A) \tag{4.7}$$

subject to $\dot{S}(A) = s(a)$, where $S(a)$ and $s(a)$ are the state and control variables, respectively.

One more modification to the maximization problem (4.7) may be required. It is now recognized in the valuation literature that individuals' WTP for certain types of environmental benefits declines with distance from the site or location, and thus WTP estimates at a specific location should be adjusted by a *distance-decay function* (Albers et al., 2008; Bateman et al., 2005; Hanley et al., 2003; Pate and Loomis, 1997). Such studies find that the WTP by individuals for benefits generated at a specific site or location tend to decline exponentially with respect to the distance of the individuals from the site. This distance-decay effect is cited as justification for including a *geographical* or *spatial discounting* term to account for how WTP varies over distance (Ando and Shah, 2009; Hannon, 1994; Perrings and Hannon, 2001). For example Perrings and Hannon (2001) show how, if pollution density evolves with the distance from the source, geographical discounting of preferences affects the optimal spatial diffusion of pollution.

In the problem considered here we have another reason to adopt spatial discounting. If ecological functions decline unidirectionally across a natural landscape, then the benefits provided by these functions will also decrease with distance. For example, as we saw previously (see Section 4.1), the benefits of storm protection and habitat-fishery linkages tend to decline with the distance inshore from the seaward edge of most coastal wetland habitats, such as mangroves and salt marshes. If the benefits of such ecosystem services decline spatially, then so would the total WTP for these service flows.

If we assume that the total WTP for ecosystem services declines at an exponential rate $e^{-\delta a}$ due to declining ecological functions across the landscape, then the maximization problem (4.7) for the total net benefits over the entire ecosystem landscape is now

$$\max_{s(a)} W = \int_0^A [V(s(a))e^{-\delta a} - m(a)s(a)]da - R(A) \qquad (4.8)$$

subject to $\dot{S}(A) = s(a)$. The Hamiltonian of the problem is

$$H = V(s(a))e^{-\delta a} - m(a)s(a) + \lambda(a)s(a),$$

where $\lambda(a)$ is the costate variable associated with the constraint and represents the marginal value of an additional unit of aggregate ecosystem services from the landscape (the marginal net benefits arising from the relaxation of the constraint, $\partial W/\partial S$).

The necessary conditions for an interior solution are (4.6) and

$$\frac{\partial H}{\partial s} = 0 \rightarrow V'(s)e^{-\delta a} - m + \lambda = 0 \tag{4.9}$$

$$\dot{\lambda} = -\frac{\partial H}{\partial S} = 0 \tag{4.10}$$

$$-R'(A) = \lambda(A) \text{ (transversality condition)} \tag{4.11}$$

From Equations (4.10) and (4.11) $\lambda(a) = \lambda^* = -R'(A)$ is a constant. The shadow aggregate value of ecosystem services is constant regardless of location, and it equals the negative of the marginal opportunity cost of holding onto the landscape, which are the foregone rents that could be earned from developing the landscape for another economic use. From Equations (4.3) and (4.4) $V'(s) = v(s) = p(a)$. Consequently, from Equation (4.9)

$$p(a)e^{-\delta a} = m(a) - \lambda^* = m(a) + R'(A). \tag{4.12}$$

The implicit price (value) of ecosystem services at landscape location a is equal to the costs of maintaining the services at that location plus the marginal opportunity cost of holding on to the entire landscape. At each location a the discounted marginal willingness to pay for the ecosystem services must be sufficiently large to offset the maintenance cost of those services at that location, $m(a)$ and the marginal opportunity cost of foregone rents from developing the entire landscape $R'(A)$. If this condition is not fulfilled, then it is optimal to covert the landscape at this location.

From Equation (4.5), at the margin $a = 0$ then $m = 0$, and thus from Equation (4.12) $p(0) = R'(A)$, which implies that the ecosystem is not worth maintaining. Differentiating Equation (4.12),

$$p'(a)e^{-\delta a} - \delta p(a)e^{-\delta a} = m'(a), \quad a > 0 \tag{4.13}$$

For $\delta = 0\, p'(a) = m'(a)$, and for $\delta > 0\, p'(a) = m'(a)e^{\delta a} + \delta p(a) > m'(a)$. The slope of $p(a)$ must be larger, when there is geographical discounting compared to the situation without. To avoid conversion occurring at any location across the landscape, the marginal WTP for ecological services at each location must be equal to their marginal maintenance cost. In fact, this is unlikely to be the case if ecosystem service benefits

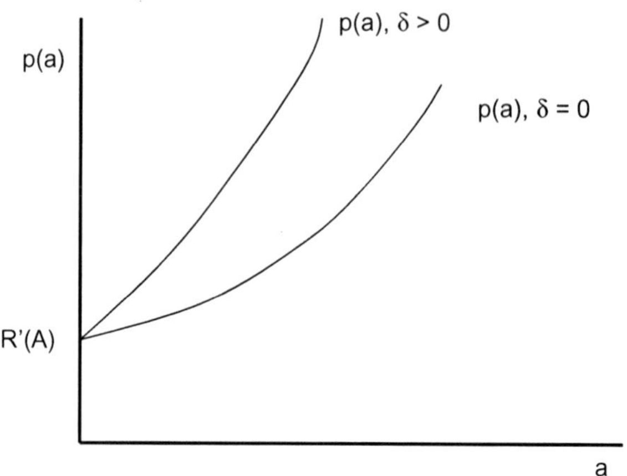

Fig. 4.3 Optimal landscape conservation across a natural landscape.

are declining at the rate δ for locations further away from the initial boundary edge of the landscape. The differences between the two cases are depicted in Figure 4.3

Although the spatial problem examined here is highly simplistic, assuming that the ecological function underlying an ecosystem service declines unidirectionally across a landscape, this example does show the importance of spatial variation in determining conservation decisions. Increasingly, economists are taking into account such considerations, and showing in particular, how the spatial variability of costs and the need for agglomeration bonuses across heterogeneous landscapes will have an important bearing on the decision as to how much land area to protect, which landscapes to include cost-effectively for achieving overall conservation targets, and the selection of alternative possible sites for protected areas (Ando et al., 1998; Balmford et al., 2003; Carwardine et al., 2008; Ferraro, 2003, 2004; Naidoo et al., 2006; Parkhurst and Shogren, 2008; Polasky et al., 2001). For example, (Ferraro, 2004, p. 907) argues that, in a given landscape, "each land parcel is a production unit, a 'manufacturing plant that produces biophysical attributes,' and these attributes can only be secured for conservation purposes through investment into a contract." As a result, "the degree to which a contracting agent can identify the 'true' cost-efficient land portfolio . . . depends on the degree to which environmental benefits ... can be measured accurately." Ferraro shows, with the example of managing a riparian buffer zone to provide water for urban residents in Syracuse, New York, that conservation investment opportunities can still be ranked without a parametric specification of the amenity function or the cost function, provided that the decision maker is at least able to identify the important biophysical and economic attributes of each landscape parcel in each location.

5

Open Economy Conditions

The purpose of this section is to show how the natural asset model is affected by introducing some simple open economy conditions. The two conditions are trade and international payment for ecosystem services. The model is extended in the most straightforward way possible, following (Barbier and Rauscher, 1994). Thus the model developed here is an abstraction from more sophisticated open economy models that consider land conversion (Barbier and Schulz, 1997; Bulte and Barbier, 2005; Hartwick et al., 2001; Jinji, 2006; Polasky et al., 2004; Smulders et al., 2004).

5.1 The Open Economy Natural Asset Model

As in the basic natural asset model of Section 3, it is assumed that an area of natural landscape, A_0, associated with an ecosystem is subject to continuous irreversible conversion to provide land for a development activity. However, following (Barbier and Schulz, 1997), it is also assumed that, given this competing land use, retaining more natural landscape would mean less land available for development activities, thus restricting aggregate production, q, from these activities.

Assuming decreasing marginal productivity of q through conversion of the natural landscape, then the aggregate production function is

$$q = f(A(t)), \quad f' < 0, \quad f'' < 0. \tag{5.1}$$

Aggregate output q is sufficiently large with respect to the entire economy that it can either be exported or consumed domestically, and the export earnings are used to import domestic consumption goods from abroad. However, the economy's exports and imports are sufficiently small with respect to world markets that the terms of trade for the economy are given. Denoting exports of aggregate output as x, then domestic consumption from land conversion activities is $q - x$. Imported consumption goods are m. With given world prices p^x for the economy's exports and p^m for its imports, then the balance of trade for the small open economy is

$$px = m, \quad p = \frac{p^x}{p^m} \tag{5.2}$$

where p represents the terms of trade for the economy's exports of aggregate production from development activities that depend on landscape conversion.

Social welfare is indicated by the utility of an infinitely lived representative consumer, whose welfare depends on domestic consumption, $q - x$, imported goods, m, and the benefit flows of ecosystem services, $B(A)$, less the costs of converting landscape, $C(c)$. The economy's objective is therefore to choose land conversion, c, and exports, x, so as to maximize the welfare function

$$W = \int_0^\infty [U(q - x, m) + B(A) - C(c)]e^{-rt}dt \tag{5.3}$$

subject to (3.4) and (5.2). It is assumed that the utility function, U, is additively separable and has the standard properties with respect to its partial derivatives, $U_i > 0$ and $U_{ii} < 0$ $(i = 1, 2)$.

The current value Hamiltonian of the problem is

$$H = U(f(A) - x, px) + B(A) - C(c) - \mu c. \tag{5.4}$$

The key necessary conditions for this problem are:

$$\frac{\partial H}{\partial x} = 0 \to U_1 - pU_2 = 0 \tag{5.5}$$

$$\frac{\partial H}{\partial c} = 0 \to \mu = -C'(c) \tag{5.6}$$

$$-\frac{\partial H}{\partial A} = \dot{\mu} - r\mu \to \dot{\mu} = r\mu - B'(A) - U_1 f'(A) \tag{5.7}$$

Condition (5.6) is the same as (3.7) for the basic natural asset model of Section 3. Condition (5.7) is similar to (3.8), although now the opportunity cost of holding on to landscape is not foregone rents but the reduced utility from less domestic consumption derived from development based on land conversion, $U_1 f'(A)$. The new condition is (5.5), which is the standard small open economy result that the relative marginal value of domestic to imported consumption must equal the fixed terms of trade.

As before, from Equations (5.6) and (5.7)

$$\mu(t) = \frac{B'(A) + \dot{\mu}}{r} + \frac{U_1 f'(A)}{r} = -C'(c) \to -\mu(t)$$

$$= P(D) - P(A) = C'(c). \tag{5.8}$$

Thus, the open economy model appears similar to the basic natural asset model. The difference between the capitalized marginal value of developed land and land retained as ecological landscape is the marginal cost of converting landscape, which also represents the difference in land prices between developed and ecological land. However, in the case of the open economy model, we can now explore what effect a change in the terms of trade might have on the optimal land conversion path of the economy. To do this, it is necessary to examine the effects on both the steady state outcome and the transition path.

5.2 A Change in the Terms of Trade

As in the basic model, in the long run steady state, $\dot{A} = \dot{\mu} = 0$. It follows that both landscape conversion and the marginal value of an additional unit of ecosystem landscape approach zero asymptotically, i.e., $c = 0$ and $\lim_{t \to \infty} \mu(t) = C_c(0) = 0$. The wedge between land prices will disappear, $P(D(t)) = P(A(t))$, and ecosystem landscape area will converge to a steady state level A^*. If the initial ecological landscape area is large $A(0) > A^*$, then along the transition path to the long run steady state, the marginal value of an additional unit of ecosystem landscape is negative $\mu < 0$, and optimal landscape conversion c is at first very large. But along the optimal path, as land conversion proceeds until the steady state is reached, $\mu(t)$ will rise and c will fall. The outcome for the optimal landscape conversion path is similar as depicted in Figure 3.1.

However, in the open economy version of the model, a change in the economy's terms of trade p will now have an impact on the both the long run steady state level of natural landscape A^* and the transition path to this equilibrium.

The steady state is determined by Equation (5.5) and, from Equation (5.7), $B'(A^*) + U_1 f'(A^*) = 0$, which are defined at the equilibrium level of natural landscape A^* and exports x^*. The comparative static effects of a change in p on these equilibrium values are

$$\frac{dx^*}{dp} = \frac{(1+\eta)\delta}{\Delta} > 0, \quad \frac{dA^*}{dp} = -\frac{(1+\eta)\gamma}{\Delta} < 0, \quad \eta = \frac{U_{22}px}{U_2},$$

$$-1 < \eta < 0, \quad \Delta = \alpha\delta - \gamma\beta < 0, \quad (5.9)$$

where $\alpha = -(U_{11} + p^2 U_{22}) > 0$, $\beta = U_{11}f'(A) > 0$, $\gamma = -U_{11}f'(A) < 0$ and $\delta = U_1 f''(A) + (f'(A))^2 U_{11} + B''(A) < 0$. Note that Δ is the determinant of the Hessian matrix of coefficients of the totally differentiated equilibrium system. This determinant is negative if $\alpha\delta < \beta\gamma$ or $-(\alpha/\gamma) < -(\beta/\delta)$, which turns out to be a necessary condition for the equilibrium to be locally stable (a saddle point).[4] Finally, η is the elasticity of the marginal utility with respect to imported goods, which reflects the degree of import dependency of the economy. As Equation (5.9) shows, under normal import dependency conditions, with $|\eta| < 1$, then we would get the result that a rise in the terms of trade would lead to more export from development activities in the long run and a lower steady state level of natural landscape.

The effect of a change in p on the transition path can be determined qualitatively through the impact on the slope of the optimal conversion

---

[4] See Barbier and Rauscher (1994) for a proof.

path. The slope of the path in the open economy is similar to that of the basic model

$$\frac{\partial \mu}{\partial A} = \frac{\dot{\mu}}{\dot{A}} = \frac{r\mu - B'(A) - U_1 f'(A)}{-c(\mu)} < 0. \qquad (5.10)$$

Although p does not appear directly on Equation (3.12), it does have an influence on this slope. From totally differentiating Equation (5.5) one gets $dp = [\alpha/(1 + \eta)]dx + [\beta/(1 + \eta)]dA$, which implies that a change in terms of trade has a positive influence on exports and natural landscape levels, given normal import dependency conditions. From totally differentiating (5.7) $d\dot{\mu} = rdu - \gamma dx - \delta dA$. Thus a rise in p causes $\mu(t)$ to rise more rapidly over time than along the original path. It follows from (5.10) that the slope of the optimal landscape conversion trajectory becomes more negative. The initial value of μ must also fall (i.e., become more negative). Initial landscape conversion must therefore be much higher, and then c declines more quickly over time. In Figure 3.1, compared to the original path, the new trajectory for $\mu(t)$ would be shifted further down. The result is that more depletion of natural landscape occurs initially, and because natural landscape area is still fixed at A_0, the result is more conversion of natural landscape in the long run too. A rise in the terms of trade speeds up initial conversion of the natural landscape, with less conservation of the ecological landscape in the long run as well.

5.3   Payment for Ecosystem Services

Now consider the possibility that the economy receives international payments for foregoing the export earnings that could otherwise be earned from development activities that require converting natural landscape. Such compensatory transfers serve indirectly as *payment for ecosystem services*, because they essentially subsidize the open economy to conserve rather than convert natural landscape, thus generating a greater flow of ecosystem services. Payments for the conservation of standing forests or wildlife habitat are the most frequent type of compensation programs used in developing countries, and they have been mainly aimed at paying landowners for the opportunity costs of preserving natural landscapes that provide one or more diverse services: carbon sequestration, watershed protection, biodiversity benefits, wildlife protection and landscape beauty (Alix-Garcia et al., 2008; Bulte et al., 2008; Grieg-Gran et al., 2005; Pagiola et al., 2005; Wunder, 2008; Zilberman et al., 2008).

In the open economy model, such international compensation payments can be represented by an increase in foreign exchange available to supplement export earnings and thus allow additional imports of consumer goods; i.e., Equation (5.2) is now

$$px + s = m, \tag{5.11}$$

and the economy's welfare function is

$$W = \int_0^\infty [U(q - x, px + s) + B(A) - C(c)]e^{-rt}dt. \tag{5.12}$$

The first-order conditions and the long-run steady state equations are unchanged for the open economy. But a change in international payments s has the following comparative static effects on the equilibrium level of natural landscape A^* and exports x^*

$$\frac{dx^*}{ds} = \frac{pU_{22}\delta}{\Delta} < 0, \quad \frac{dA^*}{ds} = -\frac{\gamma pU_{22}}{\Delta} > 0. \tag{5.13}$$

The effect of an increased payment for ecosystem services is to reduce long run exports but increase conservation of natural landscape. The payments substitute for exports and thus reduce the pressure in the long run to convert more natural landscape for development.

The slope of the optimal conversion path in the open economy is still determined by Equation (5.10), and as before, $d\dot{\mu} = rdu - \gamma dx - \delta dA$. But now, from differentiating (5.5) but keeping the terms of trade unchanged, one obtains $ds = (\alpha/pU_{22})dx + (\beta/pU_{22})dA$, which indicates that an increase in international payments has a negative influence on exports and natural landscape. Thus a rise in s causes $\mu(t)$ to increase more slowly over time than along the original path, and from Equation (5.10), the slope of the optimal landscape conversion trajectory becomes less negative. The initial value of μ must also fall (i.e., become less negative). Initial landscape conversion is therefore much lower, and c declines more slowly over time. In Figure 3.1, compared to the original path, the new trajectory for $\mu(t)$ would be shifted further in. Less depletion of natural landscape occurs initially, and in the long run less natural landscape is converted too. A rise in international payments for ecosystem services slows down initial conversion of the natural landscape, with the net result of more long run landscape conservation.

It might be tempting to conclude that, if the world community wanted to induce the small open economy to conserve more natural landscape, it could either provide more payment for ecosystem services, or alternatively, employ trade interventions that lowered the economy's terms of trade. However, recall from Section 5.3 that the effects of a change in p require that the economy have normal import dependency conditions. If instead $|\eta| > 1$, then trade interventions that lower p could actually produce counter-productive results and lead to more landscape conversion. More complex open economy models that consider land conversion often indicate that trade interventions have ambiguous impacts on conserving natural habitat (Barbier and Schulz, 1997; Bulte and Barbier, 2005; Hartwick et al., 2001; Jinji, 2006; Polasky et al., 2004; Smulders et al., 2004). Given such complications associated with trade interventions, payments for ecosystem services seem to be a preferred option for encouraging natural landscape conservation.

6

Ecological Collapse

As noted in the introduction, increasingly ecologists have identified irreversible natural landscape conversion as posing a threat of ecosystem collapse (Busing and White, 1993; Dobson et al., 2006; Lotze et al., 2006; Peterson et al., 1998; Turner et al., 1993). In this final extension of the natural asset model, we adopt the hazard rate function approach of Reed and Heras (1992) to consider this possible risk of ecological collapse. This approach was approved convenient in environmental and natural resource economics for a variety of problems in which environmental use could lead to an irrevocable change in the system, such as a fishery collapse, biological invasion, pollution, species extinction and risk of forest fire or pest damage (Amacher et al., 2009; Clarke and Reed, 1994; Knowler and Barbier, 2005; Reed, 1988; Reed and Heras, 1992; Tsur and Zemel, 1994, 2007).

6.1 Extending the Natural Asset Model to Allow for Ecological Collapse

Consider that the ecosystem is vulnerable to random catastrophic collapse as its landscape is converted irreversibly for development. Up until the collapse (if it occurs), the ecological landscape can still be converted to development activity or left to generate periodic ecosystem service flow. Thus, the net benefit flows of the allocation of ecological landscape at time t is

$$W(A, c, t) = R(A(t)) - C(c(t)) + B(A(t)). \tag{6.1}$$

As in the basic model, natural landscape conversion is governed by Equation (3.4), i.e., $\dot{A} = -c(t)$. If the instantaneous discount rate is r, then the expected net present value of the benefit flow gained up until the time of collapse is

$$J = E\left\{ \int_0^\tau W(A, c, t) e^{-rt} dt \right\} \tag{6.2}$$

where the expectation is taken with respect to the random variable τ. Maximizing Equation (6.2) with respect to Equation (3.4) is a stochastic optimization problem, which can be expressed as a problem of deterministic control by following the approach of Reed and Heras (1992) and introducing a new state variable into the problem.

The probability of collapse can be characterized by a hazard rate function that specifies the probability that the ecosystem collapses at time t, given that it has survived so far up to that time. Formally, the hazard rate can be defined as

$$h(t) = \lim_{\Delta t \to 0} \Pr(t \le T < t + \Delta t | T \ge t) / \Delta t = \frac{f(t)}{S(t)} \tag{6.3}$$

where $f(t)$ is the corresponding density function of the probability distribution of the duration T of the ecosystem $F(t) = \Pr(T < t)$. The survivor function $S(t)$ is the upper tail of this probability distribution, and it is the probability that the random variable T will equal or exceed the value t, or $S(t) = 1 - F(t) = \Pr(T \ge t)$. Note that the latter survival probability is also related to the hazard function, i.e., $S(t) = \exp\left\{ -\int_0^t h(u) du \right\}$. The latter expression can be used to introduce a new state variable

$$y(t) = -\ln S(t) = \int_0^t h(u) du. \tag{6.4}$$

The probability of ecosystem collapse, and therefore the hazard rate function, depends inversely upon the remaining ecological landscape that is not converted, i.e., from Equation (6.4)

$$\dot{y} = h(t) = \psi(A(t)), \quad \psi' < 0, \quad y(0) = 0. \tag{6.5}$$

Evaluating Equation (6.2) in terms of $y(t)$ yields

$$J = \int_0^\infty W(A,c,t)e^{-rt-y(t)}dt \tag{6.6}$$

The objective function (6.6) can now be maximized subject to the dynamic constraints (3.4) and (6.5). This is a standard problem of deterministic control similar to one that arises if there is no possibility of collapse, except for the inclusion of a new state variable $y(t)$ related to the survival function and which operates as a premium added to the discount rate. Note that $e^{-y(t)}$ is simply $S(t)$ and is often referred to as the survival probability term.

The current value Hamiltonian is

$$H = W(A,c)e^{-y(t)} - \mu_1 c + \mu_2 \psi(A), \tag{6.7}$$

which can be transformed into a conditional current value Hamiltonian by dividing H by the survival probability $e^{-y(t)}$

$$\tilde{H} = W(A,c) - \rho_1 c + \rho_2 \psi(A) \tag{6.8}$$

where $\rho_i = e^{y(t)}\mu_i$ and $\tilde{H} = He^{y(t)}$.

The first-order conditions for maximization are

$$\frac{d\tilde{H}}{dc} = \frac{dHe^{y(t)}}{dc} = 0 \rightarrow -C'(c) = \rho_1 \tag{6.9}$$

$$\dot{\rho}_1 - (\delta + \psi)\rho_1 = -\frac{d\tilde{H}}{dA} = -\frac{dHe^{y(t)}}{dA} \rightarrow \dot{\rho}_1$$

$$= [r + \psi(A)]\rho_1 - \rho_2\psi'(A) - R'(A) - B'(A) \tag{6.10}$$

$$\dot{\rho}_2 - (\delta + \psi)\rho_2 = -\frac{d\tilde{H}}{dy} = -\frac{dHe^{y(t)}}{dy} = W(A,c) \rightarrow \dot{\rho}_2$$

$$= [\delta + \psi(A)]\rho_2 + R(A) + B(A) - C(c) \tag{6.11}$$

The optimal conversion path $c^*(t)$ maximizes the conditional current-value Hamiltonian at all t, and can be found by solving the system given by conditions (6.9)–(6.10) and the dynamic equations (3.4) and (6.5). The costate variable ρ_1 is the shadow value of an additional unit of ecological landscape at time t conditional on the ecosystem not having yet collapsed at this time. As shown by Reed and Heras (1992), the costate variable ρ_2 is defined as $\rho_2 = e^{rt+y(t)}(\partial J^*/\partial y) = -V(A^*,t)$, where J^* represents the optimal value of (6.6). For the above problem, ρ_2 is therefore the negative of the expected present value at time t of the remaining optimally managed ecological landscape, given that the ecosystem has not yet collapsed. Thus $V(A^*,t)$ represents the "value" of the functioning ecosystem at time t with its landscape area at level A^*.

Interpretation of the first-order conditions is facilitated by comparing them to the case where there is no risk of ecosystem collapse. From Equation (6.11)

$$\rho_2 = \frac{\dot{\rho}_2 - W(A,c)}{\tilde{r}}, \quad \tilde{r} = (r + \psi(A)). \tag{6.12}$$

As indicated, by definition, $\rho_2 < 0$ so (6.12) must be negative. Any change in the costate variable over time must be less than the benefit flows of the ecological landscape at time t as represented by $W(A,c,t) = R(A(t)) - C(c(t)) + B(A(t))$. Both of the values on the right-hand side of Equation (6.12) are adjusted by the effective discount rate $\tilde{r}$, which includes the risk "premium" for the threat of collapse $\psi(A)$. Note that this premium implies that the effective discount rate rises as more ecological landscape is converted over time.

From Equations (6.9) and (6.10) and using $-R'(A) = R'(D)$ for annual periodic rent from developed land use

$$-R'(A) - \tilde{r}C(c) = R'(D) - \tilde{r}C(c) = B'(A) + \dot{\rho}_1 + \rho_2\psi'(A) \tag{6.13}$$

and

$$-\rho_1 = \frac{R'(D)}{\tilde{r}} - \left[\frac{B'(A) + \dot{\rho}_1}{\tilde{r}} + \frac{\rho_2\psi'(A)}{\tilde{r}}\right] = P(D) - P(A) = C'(c). \tag{6.14}$$

Expression (6.13) indicates that, once again, along the optimal landscape conversion path the returns from the two competing land uses must be equal. The marginal profits from development less conversion costs $R'(D) - \tilde{r}C(c)$ must just equal the marginal benefit of holding on to the ecological landscape $B'(A) + \dot{\rho}_1 + \rho_2\psi'(A)$. Of course now, the risk premium for collapse raises the effective discount rate and thus marginal conversion costs, $\tilde{r}C'(c)$, as more landscape is converted. In addition, the benefits of holding on to landscape include the impact of more conversion on raising the risk of collapse, $\rho_2\psi'(A)$. The latter impact is positive, implying that one would want to avoid converting more ecological landscape because it would increase the risk of collapse, which is valued in terms of the expected present value at time t of the remaining functioning ecosystem ρ_2. The change in the (conditional) shadow value of a unit of landscape $\dot{\rho}_1$ is positive and is also augmented by the growing risk of collapse from landscape conversion, since $\rho_1 = e^{y(t)}\mu_1$. Overall, Equation (6.13) implies that, with the threat of collapse posed by irreversible development of ecological landscape, along the optimal path of landscape conversion more of the ecological landscape will be preserved compared to when the threat is absent.

Expression (6.14) indicates that the difference between the capitalized marginal value of developed land and land retained as ecological landscape is again the marginal cost of converting landscape. However, the capitalized value of both land uses is determined by the effective discount rate, and thus lowered by the risk premium due to the threat of ecosystem collapse. In addition, the "price" of ecological landscape includes an additional term that, as in (6.13), reflects the impact of conversion on the increasing probability of collapse $\rho_2\psi'(A)$. The effect of this additional term plus the change in the (conditional) shadow value of a unit of landscape $\dot{\rho}_1$ is to increase the value of ecological landscape, $P(A)$. The result is that the difference in land prices between developed and ecological land will be lower than in the case without the threat of ecosystem collapse, and thus the optimal path for land conversion $c^*(t)$ is lower.

In the long run, $\dot{\rho}_1 = \dot{\rho}_2 = \dot{A} = 0$. It follows from Equations (3.4) and (6.9) that both landscape conversion and the marginal (conditional) value of an additional unit of ecosystem landscape approach zero asymptotically, i.e., $c = 0$ and $\lim_{t \to \infty} \rho_1(t) = C_c(0) = 0$. The wedge between land prices will disappear, $P(D(t)) = P(A(t))$, and ecosystem

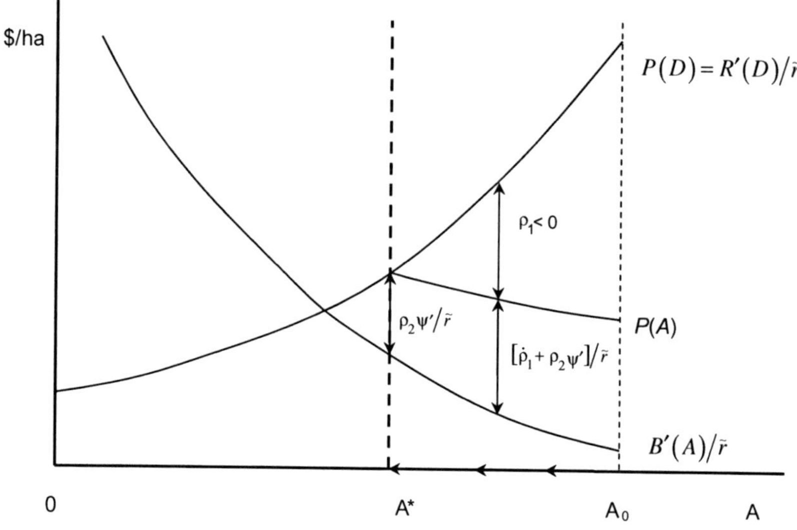

Fig. 6.1 Optimal landscape conversion with a threat of ecological collapse.

landscape area will converge to a steady state level A^*. However, from Equation (6.14), this steady-state outcome implies

$$P(D^*) = P(A^*) = \left[\frac{B'(A^*)}{\tilde{r}} + \frac{\rho_2\psi'(A^*)}{\tilde{r}} \right], \quad \rho_2 = -W(A^*). \quad (6.15)$$

Assume once again that the initial ecological landscape area is large $A(0) > A^*$. From Equation (6.9), along the transition path to the long run steady state, the marginal value of an additional unit of natural landscape, conditional on the ecosystem not yet collapsed, is negative $\rho_1 < 0$. As in the case of no threat of collapse, this conditional shadow value is rising, i.e., $\dot{\rho}_1 > 0$. Thus, optimal landscape conversion is initially large but falls over time. However, Equations (6.13) and (6.14) indicate that, along the optimal path of landscape conversion, more of the ecological landscape will be preserved compared to when the threat of collapse is absent, and thus the optimal path for land conversion $c^*(t)$ is lower due to the presence of the hazard. Finally, the steady-state level of natural landscape A^* is also larger compared to the case of no ecological collapse, as indicated by Equation (6.15).

The outcome for the optimal landscape conversion path with a risk of ecological collapse is depicted in Figure 6.1.

7

Conclusion

The purpose of this review has been to demonstrate that, by drawing on the recent literature on ecosystem services, it is possible to view ecological landscapes as natural assets that produce a flow of beneficial goods and services over time. The resulting problem of converting natural landscape or maintaining it to provide ecosystem services was expressed in terms of an economic model of competing land use. The basic natural asset model was used to illustrate a one-time irreversible development of an ecological landscape as well as continuous conversion over time. The basic model was also extended to include the possibility of an ecological transition, when it becomes technologically feasible to restore developed land as ecological landscape. Further extensions addressed how geographical variation in ecological functions affect the location and extent of natural landscape conversion in an ecosystem; how introducing open economy conditions allows consideration of terms of trade effects and international payment for ecosystem services; and finally, how irreversible landscape conversion poses a threat of ecosystem collapse.

Although the natural asset model and its extensions considered here are fairly simple and thus only illustrative, they nonetheless point to a number of important areas for further research.

First, correctly valuing non-market ecosystem services is essential for determining the optimal allocation of landscape among competing uses. By failing to value the services of ecosystems, then ecological landscapes will be undervalued as natural assets, and the result will be excessive conversion. If this loss is irreversible, then this problem is exacerbated, leading to higher user costs due to rising scarcity value of future ecosystem benefits. As we saw in Section 2.3 with the example of mangrove deforestation in Thailand by shrimp aquaculture, valuation of two important non-market ecosystem services, coastal storm protection and habitat-fishery linkages, is critical to determining mangrove land use decisions.

Second, for an ecological transition to occur, restoration must be technological feasible and that the value of a restored ecological landscape must be sufficient to justify the costs of restoration. The result is that there may be distinct phases of ecological land use, where there is an initial phase irreversible landscape conversion takes place followed by a new phase where restoration is technically and economically feasible. Such an outcome is supported by the empirical literature on some key ecosystems, and warrants further exploration by economists as to the implications for policies to encourage optimal conservation and use of natural landscapes.

Third, although economists have been developing spatial models of natural resource management, consideration of how the spatial heterogeneity of natural landscapes influences the provision of ecological functions and their services is a relatively new area in economics. Increasingly, economists have taken note of how the spatial variability of costs across heterogeneous landscapes can influence the decision as to how much land area to protect, which landscapes to include cost-effectively for achieving overall conservation targets, and the selection of alternative possible sites for protected areas. The next stage is to examine further how spatially heterogeneous landscapes influence the provision of ecosystem benefits, thus helping to identify the important biophysical and economic attributes of each landscape parcel in each location to optimize conservation decisions across ecological landscapes.

Fourth, many of the land development pressures on ecological landscapes are occurring through the need for developing economies to earn foreign exchange earnings. As explored in this review, both changes in the terms of trade and international payment for ecosystem services can influence land conversion decisions in such circumstances. More economic empirical and analytical studies are needed to verify the conditions under which an open economy is likely to conserve rather than convert natural landscape, thus generating a greater flow of ecosystem services.

Finally, large shocks or sustained disturbances to ecosystems can set in motion a series of interactions that can breach ecological thresholds that cause the systems to "flip" from one functioning state to another. Irreversible land conversion is now recognized as a major factor inhibiting the ability of an ecosystem to recover, or return, to its original state. The causes and consequences of ecological collapse have been studied by ecologists for some time, and increasingly, economists are becoming interested in how the threat of collapse affects the management of ecosystems as natural assets.

Acknowledgments

The paper has benefited from comments and suggestions by an anonymous reviewer as well as by Amy Ando, Rich Carson, Dave Finnoff, Duncan Knowler, Charles Perrings, Jason Shogren, John Tschirhart and Amos Zemel. The usual disclaimer applies, however. A version of this paper was also presented as a keynote address at the 11th Annual BioEcon Conference, "Economic Instruments to Enhance the Conservation and Sustainable Use of Biodiversity." Venice, Italy, 21–22 September 2009.

References

Aburto-Oropeza, O., E. Ezcurra, G. Danemann, V. Valdez, J. Murray, and E. Sala (2008), 'Mangroves in the Gulf of California increase fishery yields'. *Proceedings of the National Academy of Sciences* **105**(30), 10456–10459.

Aguilar-Perera, A. and R. S. Appeldoorn (2008), 'Spatial distribution of marine fishes along a cross-shelf gradient containing a continuum of mangrove-seagrass-coral reefs off southwestern Puerto Rico'. *Estuarine, Coastal and Shelf Science* **76**, 378–394.

Aksornkoae, S. and R. Tokrisnam (2004), 'Overview of shrimp farming and mangrove loss in Thailand'. In: E. B. Barbier and S. Sathirathai (eds.): *Shrimp Farming and Mangrove Loss in Thailand*. London: Edward Elgar.

Albers, H. J. (1996), 'Modeling ecological constraints on tropical forest management: Spatial interdependence, irreversibility and uncertainty'. *Journal of Environmental Economics and Management* **30**, 73–94.

Albers, H. J., A. W. Ando, and X. Chen (2008), 'A spatial-econometric analysis of attraction and repulsion of private conservation by public reserves'. *Journal of Environmental Economics and Management* **56**, 33–49.

Alix-Garcia, J. (2007), 'A spatial analysis of common property deforestation'. *Journal of Environmental Economics and Management* **53**, 141–157.

Alix-Garcia, J., A. De Janvry, and E. Sadoulet (2008), 'The role of deforestation risk and calibrated compensation in designing payments for environmental services'. *Environment and Development Economics* **13**, 375–394.

Alongi, D. M. (2008), 'Mangrove forests: Resilience, protection from tsunamis, and responses to global climate change'. *Estuarine, Coastal and Shelf Science* **76**, 1–13.

Amacher, G. S., M. Ollikainen, and E. Koskela (2009), *Economics of Forest Resources*. Cambridge, MA: MIT Press.

Ando, A. W., J. Camm, S. Polasky, and A. Solow (1998), 'Species distributions, land values, and efficient conservation'. *Science* **279**, 2126–2128.

Ando, A. W. and P. Shah (2009), 'Demand-side factors in optimal land conservation choice'. *Resource and Energy Economics,* forthcoming.

Arnott, R. J. and F. D. Lewis (1979), 'The transition of land to urban use'. *Journal of Political Economy* **87**, 161–169.

Balmford, A., K. J. Gaston, S. Blyth, A. James, and V. Kapos (2003), 'Global variation in terrestrial conservation costs, conservation benefits, and unmet conservation needs'. *Proceedings of the National Academy of Sciences* **100**, 1046–1050.

Barbier, E. B. (2001), 'A note on the economics of biological invasion'. *Ecological Economics.*

Barbier, E. B. (2003), 'Habitat-fishery linkages and mangrove loss in Thailand'. *Contemporary Economic Policy* **21**, 59–77.

Barbier, E. B. (2007), 'Valuing ecosystems as productive inputs'. *Economic Policy* **22**, 177–229.

Barbier, E. B. and J. C. Burgess (1997), 'The economics of tropical forest land use options'. *Land Economics* **73**, 174–195.

Barbier, E. B., J. C. Burgess, and A. Grainger (2009), 'The forest transition: Towards a more comprehensive theoretical framework'. *Land Use Policy,* (in press).

Barbier, E. B., E. W. Koch, B. R. Silliman, S. D. Hacker, E. Wolanski, J. H. Primavera, E. Granek, S. Polasky, S. Aswani,

L. A. Cramer, D. M. Stoms, C. J. Kennedy, D. Bael, C. V. Kappel, G. M. Perillo, and D. J. Reed (2008), 'Coastal ecosystem-based management with nonlinear ecological functions and values'. *Science* **319**, 321–323.

Barbier, E. B. and M. Rauscher (1994), 'Trade, tropical deforestation and policy interventions'. *Environmental and Resource Economics* **4**, 75–90.

Barbier, E. B. and C. E. Schulz (1997), 'Wildlife, biodiversity and trade'. *Environment and Development Economics* **2**, 145–172.

Batabyal, A. A., J. R. Kahn, and R. V. O'Neil (2003), 'On the scarcity value of ecosystem services'. *Journal of Environmental Economics and Management* **46**, 334–352.

Bateman, I. J., A. A. Lovett, and J. S. Brainard (2005), *Applied Environmental Economics: A GIS Approach to Cost-Benefit Analysis*. Cambridge: Cambridge University Press.

Benhin, J. K. A. and E. B. Barbier (2001), 'The effects of the structural adjustment program on deforestation in Ghana'. *Agricultural and Resource Economics Review* **30**, 66–80.

Bockstael, N. E. (1996), 'Modeling economics and ecology: The importance of a spatial perspective'. *American Journal of Agricultural Economics* **78**, 1168–1180.

Bosire, J. O., F. Dahdouh-Guebas, M. Walton, B. I. Crona, R. R. Lewis III, C. Field, J. G. Kairo, and N. Koedam (2008), 'Functionality of restored mangroves, a review'. *Aquatic Botany* **89**, 251–259.

Brock, W. and A. Xepapadeas (2002), 'Optimal ecosystem management when species compete for limiting resources'. *Journal of Environmental Economics and Management* **44**, 189–220.

Brown, G. and J. Roughgarden (1997), 'A metapopulation model with a common pool'. *Ecological Economics* **22**, 65–71.

Bulte, E. H. and E. B. Barbier (2005), 'Trade and renewable resources in a second-best world: An overview'. *Environmental and Resource Economics* **30**, 423–463.

Bulte, E. H., R. B. Boone, R. Stringer, and P. K. Thornton (2008), 'Elephants or onions? Paying for nature in Amboseli, Kenya'. *Environment and Development Economics* **13**, 395–414.

Busing, R. T. and P. S. White (1993), 'Effects of area on old-growth forest attributes: Implications for equilibrium landscape concept'. *Landscape Ecology* **8**, 119–126.

Carwardine, J., K. A. Wilson, G. Ceballos, P. R. Ehrlich, R. Naidoo, T. Iwamura, S. A. Hajkowicz, and H. P. Possingham (2008), 'Cost-effective priorities for global mammal conservation'. *Proceedings of the National Academy of Sciences* **105**, 11446–11450.

Clark, C. W. (1976), *Mathematical Bioeconomics*. New York: Wiley Interscience.

Clark, C. W. and G. Munro (1975), 'The economics of fishing and modern capital theory: A simplified approach'. *Journal of Environmental Economics and Management* **2**, 92–106.

Clarke, H. R. and W. J. Reed (1994), 'Consumption/pollution tradeoffs in an environment vulnerable to pollution-related catastrophic collapse'. *Journal of Economic Dynamics and Control* **18**, 991–1010.

Cochard, R., S. L. Ranamukhaarachchi, G. P. Shivakotib, O. V. Shipin, P. J. Edwards, and K. T. Seeland (2008), 'The 2004 tsunami in Aceh and Southern Thailand: A review on coastal ecosystems, wave hazards and vulnerability'. *Perspectives in Plant Ecology, Evolution and Systematics* **10**, 3–40.

Costello, C. and S. Polasky (2008), 'Optimal harvesting of stochastic spatial resources'. *Journal of Environmental Economics and Management* **56**, 1–18.

Crocker, T. D. (2005), 'Markets for conserving biodiversity habitat: Principles and practice'. In: J. F. Shogren (ed.): *Species at Risk: Using Economic Incentives to Shelter Endangered Species on Private Lands*. Austin: University of Texas Press, pp. 191–215.

Dahdouh-Guebas, F., S. Hettiarachchi, D. Lo Seen, O. Batelaan, S. Sooriyarachchi, L. P. Jayatissa, and N. Koedam (2005), 'Transitions in ancient inland freshwater resource management in Sri Lanka affect biota and human populations in and around coastal lagoons'. *Current Biology* **15**, 579–586.

Daily, G. (ed.) (1997), *Nature's Services: Societal Dependence on Natural Ecosystems*. Washington, DC: Island Press.

Dasgupta, P. S. and G. M. Heal (1974), 'The optimal depletion of exhaustible resources'. *Review of Economic Studies*, Symposium on the Economics of Exhaustible Resources, pp. 3–28.

Dasgupta, P. S. and G. M. Heal (1979), *Economic Theory and Exhaustible Resources*. Cambridge: Cambridge University Press.

Dasgupta, P. S. and K.-G. Mäler (2003), 'The economics of non-convex ecosystems: An introduction'. *Environmental and Resource Economics* **26**, 499–525.

Dobson, A., D. Lodge, J. Alder, G. S. Cumming, J. Keymer, J. McGlade, H. Mooney, J. A. Rusak, O. Sala, V. Wolters, D. Wall, R. Winfree, and M. A. Xenopoulos (2006), 'Habitat loss, trophic collapse, and the decline of ecosystem services'. *Ecology* **87**, 1915–1924.

Eichner, T. and R. Pethig (2006), 'Economic land use, ecosystem services and microfounded species dynamics'. *Journal of Environmental Economics and Management* **52**, 707–720.

Elliott, M., D. Burdon, K. L. Hemingway, and S. E. Apitz (2007), 'Estuarine, coastal and marine ecosystem restoration: Confusing management and science — a revision of concepts'. *Estuarine Coastal and Shelf Science* **74**, 349–366.

Elmqvist, T., C. Folke, M. Nyström, G. Peterson, J. Bengtsson, B. Walker, and J. Norberg (2003), 'Response Diversity, Ecosystem Change, and Resilience'. *Frontiers in Ecology and the Environment* **1**, 488–494.

Ferraro, P. J. (2003), 'Assigning priority to environmental policy interventions in a heterogeneous world'. *Journal of Policy Analysis and Management* **22**, 27–43.

Ferraro, P. J. (2004), 'Targeting conservation investments in heterogeneous landscapes: A distance-function approach and application to watershed management'. *American Journal of Agricultural Economics* **86**, 905–918.

Finnoff, D., A. Strong, and J. Tschirhart (2008), 'A bioeconomic model of cattle stocking on rangeland threatened by invasive plants and nitrogen deposition'. *American Journal of Agricultural Economics* **90**, 1074–1090.

Food and Agricultural Organization of the United Nations (FAO) (2003), 'Status and trends in mangrove area extent worldwide'. In:

M. L. Wilkie and S. Fortuna (eds.): *Forest Resources Assessment Working Paper No. 63*. Rome: Forest Resources Division, Food and Agricultural Organization of the United Nations.

Forbes, K. and J. Broadhead (2007), 'The role of coastal forests in the mitigation of tsunami impacts'. *RAP Publication 2007/1*, Bakgkok: Food and Agricultural Organization of the United Nations, Regional Office for Asia and the Pacific.

Gaudet, G., M. Moreaux, and S. Salant (2001), 'Intertemporal depletion of resource sites by spatially distributed users'. *American Economic Review* **91**, 1149–1159.

Grainger, A. (1995), 'The forest transition: An alternative approach'. *Area* **27**, 242–251.

Grainger, A. (2008), 'Difficulties in tracking the long-term global trend in tropical forest area'. *Proceedings of the National Academy of Sciences* **105**, 818–823.

Grieg-Gran, M.-A., I. Porras, and S. Wunder (2005), 'How can market mechanisms for forest environmental services help the poor? Preliminary lessons from Latin America'. *World Development* **33**, 1511–1527.

Hanley, N. and E. Barbier (2009), *Pricing Nature: Cost-Benefit Analysis and Environmental Policy*. Cheltenham, London: Edward Elgar.

Hanley, N., F. Schläpfer, and J. Spurgeon (2003), 'Aggregating the benefits of environmental improvements: Distance-decay functions for use and non-use values'. *Journal of Environmental Management* **68**, 297–304.

Hannon, B. (1994), 'Sense of place: Geographical discounting by people, animals and plants'. *Ecological Economics* **26**, 157–174.

Hartman, R. (1976), 'The harvesting decision when the standing forest has value'. *Economic Inquiry* **14**, 52–58.

Hartwick, J., N. von Long, and H. Tian (2001), 'Deforestation and development in a small open economy'. *Journal of Environmental Economics and Management* **41**, 235–251.

Heal, G. M., E. Barbier, K. Boyle, A. Covich, S. Gloss, C. Hershner, J. Hoehn, S. Polasky, C. Pringle, K. Segerson, and K. Shrader-Frechette (2005), Valuing *Ecosystem Services: Toward Better*

Environmental Decision Making. Washington, DC: The National Academies Press.

Holling, C. S. (1973), 'Resilience and stability of ecological systems'. *Annual Review of Ecological Systems* **4**, 1–23.

Jinji, N. (2006), 'International trade and terrestrial open-access renewable resources in a small open economy'. *Canadian Journal of Economics* **39**, 790–808.

Just, R. E., D. L. Hueth, and A. Schmitz (2004), *The Welfare Economics of Public Policy: A Practical Approach to Project and Policy Evaluation*. Cheltenham, UK: Edward Elgar.

Kareiva, P., S. Watts, R. McDonald, and T. Boucher (2007), 'Domesticated nature: Shaping landscapes and ecosystems for human welfare'. *Science* **316**, 1866–1869.

Kauppi, P. E., J. H. Ausubel, J. Fang, A. S. Mather, R. A. Sedjo, and P. E. Waggoner (2006), 'Returning forests analyzed with the forest identity'. *Proceedings of the National Academy of Sciences* **103**, 17574–17579.

Knowler, D. J. and E. B. Barbier (2005), 'Importing exotic plants and the risk of invasion: Are market-based instruments adequate?'. *Ecological Economics* **52**, 341–354.

Kolstad, C. (1994), 'Hotelling rents in hotelling space: Product differentiation in exhaustible resource markets'. *Journal of Environmental Economics and Management* **26**, 163–180.

Krutilla, J. V. and A. C. Fisher (1985), *The Economics of Natural Environments: Studies in the Valuation of Commodity and Amenity Resources*. Washington, DC: Resources for the Future.

Levin, S. (1999), *Fragile Dominion: Complexity and the Commons*. Reading, MA: Perseus Books.

Lewis III, R. R. (2000), 'Ecologically based goal setting in mangrove forest and tidal marsh restoration in Florida'. *Ecological Engineering* **15**, 191–198.

Lewis III, R. R. (2005), 'Ecological engineering for successful management and restoration of mangrove forests'. *Ecological Engineering* **24**, 403–418.

Lewis III, R. R. and R. G. Gilmore Jr (2007), 'Important considerations to achieve successful mangrove forest restoration with optimum fish habitat'. *Bulletin of Marine Science* **3**, 823–837.

Lotze, H. K., H. S. Lenihan, B. J. Bourque, R. H. Bradbury, R. G. Cooke, M. C. Kay, S. M. Kidwell, M. X. Kirby, C. H. Peterson, and J. B. C. Jackson (2006), 'Depletion, degradation and recovery potential of estuaries and coastal seas'. *Science* **312**, 1806–1809.

Manson, F. J., N. R. Loneragan, G. A. Skilleter, and S. R. Phinn (2005), 'An evaluation of the evidence for linkages between mangroves and fisheries: A synthesis of the literature and identification of research directions'. *Oceanography and Marine Biology: An Annual Review* **43**, 483–513.

Mather, A. S. (1992), 'The forest transition'. *Area* **24**, 367–379.

Mather, A. S. (2000), 'South-North challenges in global forestry'. In: M. Palo and H. Vanhanen (eds.): *World Forests from Deforestation to Transition?* Dordrecht: Kluwer, pp. 25–40.

Mather, A. S. (2007), 'Recent Asian forest transitions in relation to forest transition theory'. *International Forestry Review* **9**, 491–502.

May, R. M. (1975), *Stability and Complexity in Model Ecosystems.* NJ: Princeton University Press, 2nd edition.

Mazda, Y., M. Magi, M. Kogo, and P. N. Hong (1997), 'Mangroves as a coastal protection from waves in the Tong King Delta, Vietnam'. *Mangroves and Salt Marshes* **1**, 127–135.

McConnell, K. E. (1989), 'The optimal quantity of land in agriculture'. *Northeast Journal of Agricultural and Resource Economics*, October pp. 63–72.

Meynecke, J.-O., S. Y. Lee, and N. C. Duke (2008), 'Linking spatial metrics and fish catch reveals the importance of coastal wetland connectivity to inshore fisheries in Queensland, Australia'. *Biological Conservation* **141**, 981–996.

Millennium Ecosystem Assessment (2005), *Ecosystems and Human Well-being: A Framework for Assessment.* Washington, DC: Island Press.

Murray, J. D. (1993), *Mathematical Biology.* Berlin: Springer-Verlag.

Naidoo, R., A. Balmford, P. J. Ferraro, S. Polasky, T. H. Ricketts, and M. Roget (2006), 'Integrating economic costs into conservation planning'. *TRENDS in Ecology and Evolution* **21**, 681–687.

O'Neill, R. V. (2001), 'Is it time to bury the ecosystem concept? (With full military honors, of course!)'. *Ecology* **82**, 3275–3284.

Pagiola, S., A. Arcenas, and G. Platais (2005), 'Can payments for environmental services help reduce poverty? An exploration of the issues and the evidence to date from Latin America'. *World Development* **33**(2), 237–253.

Pagiola, S., K. von Ritter, and J. Bishop (2004), *How Much is an Ecosystem Worth? Assessing the Economic Value of Conservation.* Washington, DC: The World Bank.

Palo, M. and H. Vanhanen (eds.) (2000), *World Forests from Deforestation to Transition?* Dordrecht: Kluwer.

Parkhurst, G. M. and J. F. Shogren (2008), 'Smart subsidies for conservation'. *American Journal of Agricultural Economics* **90**, 1192–1200.

Parks, P. J. (1995), 'Explaining 'irrational' land use: Risk aversion and marginal agricultural land'. *Journal of Environmental Economics and Management* **28**, 34–47.

Parks, P. J., E. B. Barbier, and J. C. Burgess (1998), 'The economics of forest land use in temperate and tropical areas'. *Environmental and Resource Economics* **11**, 473–487.

Pate, J. and J. B. Loomis (1997), 'The effect of distance on willingness to pay values: A case study of wetlands and salmon in California'. *Ecological Economics* **20**, 199–207.

Perrings, C. (1998), 'Resilience in the dynamics of economic-environmental systems'. *Environmental and Resource Economics* **11**, 503–520.

Perrings, C. and B. Hannon (2001), 'An introduction to spatial discounting'. *Journal of Regional Science* **41**, 23–38.

Perry, G. L. W. (2002), 'Landscapes, space and equilibrium: Shifting viewpoints'. *Progress in Physical Geography* **26**, 339–359.

Petersen, J. E., W. M. Kemp, R. Bartleson, W. R. Boynton, C.-C. Chen, J. C. Cornwell, R. H. Gardner, D. C. Hinkle, E. D. Houde, T. C. Malone, W. R. Mowitt, L. Murray, L. P. Sanford, J. C. Stevenson, K. L. Sundberg, and S. E. Suttles (2003), 'Multiscale experiments in coastal ecology: Improving realism and advancing theory'. *BioScience* **53**, 1181–1197.

Peterson, G., C. R. Allen, and C. S. Holling (1998), 'Ecological resilience, biodiversity and scale'. *Ecosystems* **1**, 6–18.

Peterson, G. W. and R. E. Turner (1994), 'The value of salt marsh edge vs interior as habitat for fish and decapods crustaceans in a Louisiana tidal marsh'. *Estuaries* **17**, 235–262.

Pickett, S. T. A. and M. L. Cadenasso (1995), 'Landscape ecology: Spatial heterogeneity in ecological systems'. *Science* **269**, 331–334.

Pickett, S. T. A. and M. L. Cadenasso (2002), 'The ecosystem as a multidimensional concept: Meaning, model, and metaphor'. *Ecosystems* **5**, 1–10.

Pimm, S. L. (1984), 'The complexity and stability of ecosystems'. *Nature* **307**, 321–326.

Polasky, S., J. D. Camm, and B. Garber-Yonts (2001), 'Selecting biological reserves cost-effectively: An application to terrestrial vertebrate conservation in Oregon'. *Land Economics* **77**, 68–78.

Polasky, S., C. Costello, and C. McAusland (2004), 'On trade, land-use and biodiversity'. *Journal of Environmental Economics and Management* **48**, 911–925.

Reed, D. J. and L. Wilson (2004), 'Coast 2050: A new approach to restoration of Louisiana coastal wetlands'. *Physical Geography* **25**, 4–21.

Reed, W. J. (1988), 'Optimal harvesting of a fishery subject to random catastrophic collapse'. *IMA Journal of Mathematics Applied in Medicine and Biology* **5**, 215–235.

Reed, W. J. and H. E. Heras (1992), 'The conservation and exploitation of vulnerable resources'. *Bulletin of Mathematical Biology* **54**, 185–207.

Robinson, E. J. Z., H. J. Albers, and J. C. Williams (2008), 'Spatial and temporal modeling of community non-timber forest extraction'. *Journal of Environmental Economics and Management* **56**, 234–245.

Rountree, R. A. and K. W. Able (2007), 'Spatial and temporal habitat use patterns for salt marsh nekton: Implications for ecological functions'. *Aquatic Ecology* **41**, 25–45.

Rowthorn, B. and G. M. Brown (1999), 'When a high discount rate encourages biodiversity'. *International Economic Review* **40**, 315–332.

Rudel, T. K., O. T. Coomes, E. Moran, F. Achard, A. Angelsen, J. Xu, and E. Lambin (2005), 'Forest transitions: Towards a global understanding of land use change'. *Global Environmental Change* 15, 23–31.

Sanchirico, J. and J. Wilen (1999), 'Bioeconomics of spatial exploitation in a patchy environment'. *Journal of Environmental Economics and Management* 37, 129–150.

Sanchirico, J. and J. Wilen (2005), 'Optimal spatial management of renewable resources: Matching policy scope to ecosystem scale'. *Journal of Environmental Economics and Management* 50, 23–46.

Sathirathai, S. and E. Barbier (2001), 'Valuing mangrove conservation, Southern Thailand'. *Contemporary Economic Policy* 19, 109–122.

Scheffer, M., S. Carpenter, J. A. Foley, C. Folke, and B. Walker (2001), 'Catastrophic shifts in ecosystems'. *Nature* 413, 591–596.

Scott, A. (1955), 'The fishery: The objectives of sole ownership'. *Journal of Political Economy* 63, 116–124.

Shoup, D. C. (1970), 'The optimal timing of urban land development'. *Papers of the Regional Science Association* 25, 33–44.

Simenstad, C., D. Reed, and M. Ford (2006), 'When is restoration not? Incorporating landscape-scale processes to restore self-sustaining ecosystems in coastal wetland restoration'. *Ecological Engineering* 26, 27–39.

Smith, M. D., J. N. Sanchirico, and J. E. Wilen (2009), 'The economics of spatial-dynamic processes: Applications to renewable resources'. *Journal of Environmental Economics and Management* 57, 104–121.

Smith, V. L. (1968), 'Economics of production from natural resources'. *American Economic Review* 77, 1810–198.

Smulders, S., D. van Soest, and C. Withagen (2004), 'International trade, species diversity, and habitat conservation'. *Journal of Environmental Economics and Management* 48, 891–910.

Stavins, R. N. and A. B. Jaffe (1990), 'Unintended impacts of public investments on private decisions: The depletion of forested wetlands'. *American Economic Review* 80, 337–352.

Takayama, A. (1994), *Analytical Methods in Economics*. New York: Harvester Wheatsheaf.

Tokrisna, R. (1998), 'The use of economic analysis in support of development and investment decision in Thai aquaculture: With particular reference to marine shrimp culture'. A report to the Food and Agriculture Organization of the United Nations, Rome.

Tschirhart, J. (2000), 'General equilibrium of an ecosystem'. *Journal of Theoretical Biology* **203**, 13–32.

Tsur, Y. and A. Zemel (1994), 'Endangered species and natural resource exploitation: Extinction vs Coexistence'. *Journal of Economic Dynamics and Control* **20**, 1289–1305.

Tsur, Y. and A. Zemel (2007), 'Bio-economic resource management under threats of environmental catastrophes'. *Ecological Research* **22**, 431–438.

Turner, M. G. (2005), 'Landscape ecology: What is the state of the science?'. *Annual Reviews of Ecological and Evolutionary Systems* **36**, 319–344.

Turner, M. G., W. H. Romme, R. H. Gardner, R. V. O'Neill, and T. K. Kratz (1993), 'A revised concept of landscape equilibrium: Disturbance and stability on scaled landscapes'. *Landscape Ecology* **8**, 213–227.

UNEP (2006), 'Marine and coastal ecosystems and human well-being: A synthesis report based on the findings of the Millennium Ecosystem Assessment'. United Nations Environment Programme, Nairobi.

Valiela, I., J. Bowen, and J. York (2001), 'Mangrove forests: One of the world's threatened major tropical environments'. *BioScience* **51**, 807–815.

Walker, R. T. (1993), 'Deforestation and economic development'. *Canadian Journal of Regional Science* **16**, 481–497.

Wolanski, E. (2007), *Estuarine Ecohydrology*. Amsterdam: Elsevier.

World Resources Institute (2001), *World Resources 2001. People and Ecosystems: The Fraying Web of Life*. Washington, DC: World Resources Institute.

Worm, B., E. B. Barbier, N. Beaumont, J. E. Duffy, C. Folke, B. S. Halpern, J. B. C. Jackson, H. K. Lotze, F. Micehli, S. R. Palumbi, E. Sala, K. A. Selkoe, J. J. Stachowicz, and R. Watson (2006), 'Impacts of biodiversity loss on ocean ecosystem services'. *Science* **314**, 787–790.

Wunder, S. (2008), 'Payments for environmental services and the poor: Concepts and preliminary evidence'. *Environment and Development Economics* **13**, 279–297.

Zilberman, D., L. Lipper, and N. McCarthy (2008), 'When could payments for environmental services benefit the poor?'. *Environment and Development Economics* **13**, 255–278.

Zonneveld, I. S. (1989), 'The land unit — A fundamental concept in landscape ecology, and its applications'. *Landscape Ecology* **3**, 67–86.

LaVergne, TN USA
04 December 2009
166011LV00002B/1/P